The

Intelligent

Heart

The

Intelligent

Heart

Transform Your Life with the Laws of Love

by David McArthur & Bruce McArthur

ARE
PRESS

ASSOCIATION FOR
RESEARCH AND
ENLIGHTENMENT

A.R.E. Press • Virginia Beach • Virginia

A.R.E. Press
215 67th Street
Virginia Beach, VA 23451-2061

Library of Congress Cataloging-in-Publication Data
McArthur, David (David Metz)
    The intelligent heart / David McArthur and Bruce McArthur.
        p.   cm.
    Includes bibliographical references.
    ISBN 0-87604-389-9 (pbk.)
    1. Spiritual life. 2. Association for Research and Enlightenment. I.
McArthur, Bruce, 1918-1995. II. Title
BP605.A77M37   1997
291.4'4—dc21   97-2180

Cover Design by Lightbourne Images

DEDICATION

This book is dedicated to Bruce McArthur. His lifelong quest to understand the Universal Laws is its foundation, and his commitment to living the law is its soul. Its heart is his care for others from which his pioneering effort to bring the law into written form sprang. As you live the law, you become the law. I was blessed to be son and student for which I am deeply grateful.

CONTENTS

Acknowledgments

My wife, Kathryn, through her patience, faith, and love has been a tremendous source of strength and encouragement without which this book would not have come into manifestation. Our children, Lisa, Peter, and Anna, have been my teachers of the law over many years and a tremendous source of love, joy, and fulfillment.

There are many people whose care and contributions have touched this book over many years. My sincere gratitude for contributions in many forms to Cheryl Ramos, Helen Pohlman, Shirley Keller, and Thora and Weaver Hess. Special thanks to Deborah Rozman, Sara Paddison, and Doc Lew Childre for their contributions, support, and inspiration, and to all the HeartMath staff for demonstrating the power, intelligence, and warmth of the heart so well. Thanks also to Kieth VonderOhe and Kathleen Prata for their editing talents.

There are many people who have studied the laws and shared their life experiences with me, thus assisting my understanding to unfold. To those whose life experiences are reported here, whether directly or indirectly, my heart is deeply grateful to you.

My support, inspiration, and teacher was my father Bruce, who is author with me. His work in bringing the laws into clear expression has been an inspiration to my living as well as this writing. My mother, Charlotte McArthur, has been a constant support to both of us, joining in our exploration and lifting our thinking and understanding to another level. She is as much a creator of this work at every level as either of us.

Truly I have been deeply blessed to learn the laws in the company of such marvelous beings.

Introduction

Dear Reader,

I bring you a gift that has been given to me. The first part of this gift was an understanding of how we actually create our lives. I received this part of the gift quite some time ago, and I found it very frustrating. I came to realize that my real desire was not satisfied with understanding how I had created my life. What I really wanted to know was how to transform the life I had created. It is the understanding of transformation, the second part of the gift, that has been of real value to me. This is what I hope to share with you through this work in some small way.

This book is a fulfillment of many wonderful things that have unfolded in my life all of which kept leading me deeper and deeper into the study and experience of the Universal Laws. My interest in the process of human transformation took me into a comprehensive examination of these laws. In that I had the support, mentoring, and encouragement of both Bruce and Charlotte McArthur, my parents. To have their support and companionship in this search brought to it a richness and acceleration that I could not have found on my own. We often opened and explored many different ways of knowledge and perception. Bringing them back to our common experience and knowledge kept me from becoming lost in the pure mass of spiritual concepts with their varied levels of consciousness.

The pioneer in this work was Bruce McArthur. He recognized that the insights found in the readings of the psychic Edgar Cayce were far beyond the level of spiritual knowledge that we were finding in the many great spiritual leaders and teachers we were reading. There is, in addition to the exceptionally high quality of Cayce's psychic gift, a singular reason for the excellence we found. Cayce's knowledge was focused on application. He was responding to people with real questions, difficulties and challenges in their lives, and utilizing the knowledge he accessed to help them meet those challenges head on. This creates the problem of working with the Cayce material, in that it is not a coherent lecture explaining concepts to the student; every situation is personal to the individual who requested assistance. The great benefit is that we are not looking at material that is theoretical but at material that is meant to be used, applied, and lived. The key to extracting the wisdom of those readings has been the years of research which Bruce and Charlotte invested in the readings. The last time I looked in the study in their house, I found at least six tall file cabinets and many shelves filled with their Cayce research, plus many books of spiritual wisdom from all paths.

I have joined them in that endeavor and have sought to test the laws as I understood them. The ultimate test of these laws for me has been to assist people in applying them and observe if the laws brought actual transformation for ordinary people. A few of those experiences are shared here.

These experiences, with people applying the Laws of Transformation, primarily through their love, have been deeply rewarding and powerful beyond what I am able to portray in the descriptions of this book. Most of those experiences are confidential so I have not been able to share them with you. Some were repeated so often that they are represented here as composite stories rather than the experience of any single individual. Where I have related situations with accurate names, those individuals have expressed their willingness to share their experiences with you. As I witnessed people living and applying the laws while testing them in my own life, their order and clarity became readily apparent. It is from those observations of life, as much as from the research into others' perspectives, that I share this understanding of the Laws of Transformation with you.

In our research we discovered that many teachers mention the laws, although very few bring definition or categorization to them. We have chosen to learn from the knowledge of those that have, without integrating the different labels and definitions together. That would be a separate work in itself. In most cases we have utilized the classifications we found within the Cayce readings. In others, we have used the title and definition we believed would be most accurate for the reader's understanding.

The first delineation of these Universal Laws was set out in Bruce's book, *Your Life: Why It Is the Way It Is and What You Can Do About It*, also published by A.R.E. Press. That work focused primarily on the Laws of Cause and Effect. These are the laws through which we create most of our life experience. They operate through our thoughts, feelings, beliefs, and actions. It is my hope that you will study also *Your Life*. While working extensively with the Laws of Cause and Effect, Bruce and I developed an understanding of the importance of the Laws of Transformation. It is through these great transformative laws that we find fulfillment and accomplish the leaps in consciousness that free us from the world's limitations and give rise to our highest creations. This book is about these wonderful laws and the amazing experience of love that is their power source.

In the last several years, our understanding of the laws took a quantum leap as we began working with Doc Lew Childre and his Institute of HeartMath in Boulder Creek, California. Childre has been developing the solid scientific data that takes transformation out of myth and into reality. His understanding of the laws and the dimensional nature of their operation has been invaluable to us. He has helped us to drop many concepts that limited our view of the power of the Laws of Transformation and assisted us in learning the true nature of their operation through testing them in our own lives. Through the application of his wisdom, he simplified the application of these complex laws.

Bruce and I worked on this book separately for some time. We then began the fine-tuning of our writing to unite it in one volume when the book was interrupted by the sudden acceleration of a cancer Bruce had been dealing with for some years. In hindsight his experience of this disease, that resulted in his transition from the earth plane, provided our family with the opportunity to learn the application of these laws in one of their highest forms. Part of the gift of that time was the understanding that this pattern within his body was not a karmic creation but rather his soul's choice for the completion of his life's journey.

Preparing this book also gave me the very special gift of going through my father's writing and bringing his insights of inner and outer study to you. This book is indeed "our" work. Our individual contributions are interwoven throughout. Except where Bruce recounts some personal incidents, I have kept the first person style without differentiating the speaker. We have both explored each of these laws at depth and would easily speak of them with one accord.

From both of our hearts we offer to you these simple, yet truly powerful laws that hold the potential of creating a life experience of tremendous meaning, joy, and fulfillment. Enjoy.

David McArthur
June 1997

Usage of the Edgar Cayce Readings

The Association for Research and Enlightenment, Inc. (A.R.E.), is a membership organization for those interested in the study and use of the Cayce readings.

For reference purposes and to preserve anonymity, each person who received a reading was given a number, and the reading carries that number instead of the name of the person. For example, reading number 3902-2 was given for the person assigned number 3902. The particular reading was the second one that the person obtained from Cayce, as indicated by the "-2" following the reading number.

In giving readings, Cayce sometimes used archaic biblical language. In order to make these easier to understand, we have received A.R.E. approval to substitute modern English language equivalents for the archaic words. These substitutions do not change the meaning of the message. In those cases the reference reading number is followed by the designation AR for "Archaic Revised."

In some cases I have, for clarity, paraphrased a reading. The reading number in that case is followed by P for "paraphrased."

Chapter 1

The Universal Laws

When such Ahimsa (pure love) becomes all-embracing, it transforms everything it touches. There is no limit to its power.

M.K. Gandhi[1]

IS THERE ORDER IN MY CHAOS?

The concept that laws govern life is not new. This thought underlies the scientific paradigm which studies the order of the physical world and how things relate through a system of laws. But what about the events and experiences of our lives and how they relate to each other? Are those also governed by laws? Are there causes for the events in our lives that are within our control? Are we the architects of our lives or simply occupants?

For ages we human beings have believed that we play a role in our destiny. We have seen that the quality and nature of our actions determine the kind of lives we experience. And yet there are many questions that arise when we look at what happens to us in life. Was I causing all this or was I one of the countless victims of life's whims? If I was the determining factor in what happened to me, how could I have responded so that life got better and some of my desires were fulfilled? These questions have fascinated me and become a major focus of study in my life.

There are many references to laws that govern our lives. Sacred literature, the writings of mystics, philosophers, and many

1

aspects of folk wisdom have acknowledged the existence of these laws. The readings of the psychic Edgar Cayce are also a very unique body of information that allows a deeper examination of this concept of laws. From Mr. Cayce's trance state he diagnosed illnesses, suggested cures, and described causative physical conditions for people's illnesses. He also explained to people how their life experiences were the result of their interactions with what he said were laws that governed their lives. He described Universal Laws, what they were, and how they applied to each individual's life situation. His readings gave me the opportunity to look at these laws as they were operating in the lives of people meeting the everyday challenges of life.

I began studying the Universal Laws through the Cayce readings and the writings of other great teachers to answer some of my questions as to "why" things happened in our lives. What caused our successes and our failures, our joys and our happinesses? Indeed the Universal Laws did explain how we create our lives. As those understandings became clear, I discovered that there was a much greater gift given by the knowledge of these laws—the knowledge of how to transform any situation we may find in our lives into one of meaning and fulfillment. This transformation is a result of a fundamental shift in perception about an experience. That shift can be so profound that people have been able to change a situation that appears debilitating into one that is meaningful and empowering.

This fundamental change is possible through a specific set of laws—the Laws of Transformation. Edgar Cayce described many of these Laws of Transformation and assisted individuals in applying them in a way that lifted the quality of their life experience. In the following reading excerpt, he describes for an individual how working with these laws leads to personal growth and new opportunity.

> Let the law of the *Lord*, as *thou knowest* it in thine heart,
> *be* the *rule* of *thy* life—and thy dealings with thy fellow man!
> And ye will find that the growth of the mind-spiritual, of the
> mind-mental, of the body-physical, will open the way for
> thee, day by day.[2] (601-11)

It is these laws, the Laws of Transformation, that this book is primarily about. However, we will also touch upon a more basic level of law, called the Laws of Cause and Effect, in order to understand why or how a situation is created. Through the Laws of Cause and Effect, we can understand our role in creating our lives. However, it is the Laws of Transformation that give us the bail-out—the way out of difficulties and limitations we have created in our lives. They provide the opportunity in any experience to obtain a higher, more meaningful perspective that moves us through our difficulties and brings fulfillment into our experience.

In recent years, a major contribution has been made to the understanding of the Laws of Transformation and how they operate. This new contribution comes from recent breakthroughs in science that describe the changes that occur in our physiological, psychological, and electromagnetic systems as we apply the Laws of Transformation. In addition to the subjective changes we experience in feeling, perspective, clarity, and intelligence, we can also see the objective data of these transformational changes in our heart rate, blood pressure, respiratory system, immune system, and our electromagnetic spectrum.

The archetypal images of our folk literature, the great minds of the world's greatest teachers, the psychic abilities of people like Edgar Cayce, and the discoveries of modern science help us understand how to discern these laws that transform our lives. But the real test of these laws is not someone else's knowledge. The real test of these laws is your own life. As this book describes these laws and the techniques to apply them, be your own self-scientist and put them to the test. Do they transform your experience?

Edgar Cayce described this test that I believe we all must make as we learn about life and how to live it. He said,

> . . .for to Him, to His laws, must all come; the nearer we apply them . . . the greater blessings to self, the greater may be the blessings *of* self upon others. (2906-1)AR

UNIVERSAL LAWS

One of the important understandings of the Universal Laws is that they are not haphazard. The laws are as dependable and immutable as the laws of physics. They always work.

A Universal Law is a principle of creation that operates in all phases of humankind's life and existence, for all human beings everywhere, all the time.[3]

An example of a Universal Law operating at a physical level is the refraction of light through a prism. As I sit here the sunlight is coming in through my window where a prism is sitting. The laws of optics operate to break up that stream of light and project it as the rainbow colors of the spectrum upon my wall. I can work with the laws of optics to increase the clarity of the rainbows by the cleanliness and quality of the prism I use. The prism works the same for my little daughter who does not understand the laws of optics. When she holds it in the light, the rainbows appear.

Because of my knowledge, I know to put it by the window, to dust it off, and to position it, but it does not respond to me because I am good or bad, wise or foolish. It does not judge my motives. It operates because the laws of optics are a part of the Universal Laws and operate the same for every person, everywhere, all the time.

In this book, we are examining the Universal Laws through which we create our experiences of life. Many people have never heard about Universal Laws and would probably dispute their existence. Such was also the case with the laws of optics at one time. It makes no difference to the law. It operates perfectly in our lives whether we believe in it or not. Unlike manmade laws, we cannot set these aside. They always work. Our choice is whether or not to learn about them and use them constructively in our lives.

LAWS OF CAUSE AND EFFECT

In discovering how to apply the Laws of Transformation, it is helpful to know how the Universal Laws bring our life experiences into manifestation. This is something that many people are aware of in a casual way. We have all acknowledged the operation of the basic building blocks of our lives, the Laws of Cause and Effect. We have acknowledged the law of "Like begets like" with the statement "What goes around comes around" and the operation of "Like attracts like" with "Birds of a feather flock together."

We teach our children attributes of character because we know that the qualities of their personalities will determine the quality of their life experience. We tell countless stories with moral teachings illustrating our belief that our actions determine how we are treated. We hold in high regard teachings such as the golden rule, "Do unto others as you would have them do unto you," because we realize this is in fact what happens. These beliefs are not limited to our Western culture, but are found throughout the world.

Although the acknowledgment of such laws in our society is extensive, there are very few attempts to list these laws and their relationship to each other. One such work is *Your Life*, which explains these basic Laws of Cause and Effect in depth, as well as their relationship to the Laws of Transformation. Let's look at two of these most basic laws.

THE LAW OF BEGETTING
"Like begets like."

He who does not trust enough will not be trusted.

They do not quarrel, so no one quarrels with them.

The sage never tries to store things up.
The more he does for others, the more he has.
The more he gives to others, the greater his abundance.

Lao Tsu

Just as chickens beget chickens and horses beget horses, so our actions beget similar actions that we find returning to our lives. In its simplest sense the Law of Begetting assures that what we do to another will be done to us. Actions we take will at some time be returned to us, emotions we express will be expressed to us, and conditions we create for another will be experienced by us. It also is the force through which feelings, thoughts, and beliefs we hold within ourselves become a part of our life experience. This law determines many of the actions, things, attitudes, and conditions that are a part of our present life situations.

Remember—these are as the unchangable laws:
As you do to others, it comes back to you. As you would that others should do to you, do to them.
This applies whether in family or with just an acquaintance, or associates of any kind. (1688-9)AR

We have all experienced extending our genuine friendship to someone and having that friendship returned. Yet we can also think of people to whom we were friendly, and they were not friendly in return. We have all given love and had love returned, but there are also people we have loved who did not love us back. The law does not say that the person to whom we express an action or attitude will bring it back to us. It only says that it will come back. In this law, there is often a time delay.

HAROLD

Harold was a classmate of mine who was scheduled to do some practice teaching. He did an excellent presentation and asked for questions. Harold stared, unbelieving, as a classmate responded to his class presentation with a sudden burst of anger that seemed totally out of place. "I wonder what caused that?" he said to me after the class. He probably meant, "I wonder what was wrong with my classmate?" Harold thought the outburst was so unreasonable that he had had no part in it at all. He was merely its victim.

I thought back to about half an hour before the class when Harold was thinking about his upcoming presentation. In his concentration he was unaware of the joking around that was taking place among his friends. One of the friends pulled on Harold's chair as Harold sat down. Harold immediately responded with a burst of harsh anger toward the friend that was inappropriate for the circumstances. As I reflected on the experience, I recognized that the irrational reaction and even the intensity of that moment were returned to Harold in the same degree that he had expressed sixty minutes earlier.

Harold experienced the Law of Begetting, which brought to him the same type of reaction that he had conveyed to his friend. Through the Law of Begetting attitudes or actions we express to others return to us by someone whose mental and emotional pattern contains a similar component to the one to which we gave expression.

THE LAW OF ATTRACTION
"Like attracts like."

Remember being in a room when someone entered filled with joy and happiness? Almost everyone in the room began feeling and expressing greater joy and happiness. It was as if the joy of one person attracted the joy in others to the surface. People would laugh, smile, or share a happy comment.

I remember working in an office on a day that I was feeling angry. A woman entered who was always happy and positive. She talked joyously with several people. I dreaded the thought that she might speak to me. Her vibration of joy was inconsistent with my vibration of negativity. I could feel my joy being pulled forth. This was the Law of Attraction at work. Because I didn't want to give up my negative mood, I felt a real desire to get away from her influence. I found an excuse to go work somewhere else for a while.

This is a simple example of the Law of Attraction. It happens so often that we view it as commonplace. We are drawn to people with similar attitudes and interests. The people who like to gossip tend to sit together, the sports people sit together, the hunters and the philosophers each find their own groups. As the saying goes, "Birds of a feather flock together."

The Law of Attraction is described in its simplest form as "Like attracts like." I also think of this law as the Law of Reflection. By understanding this law, we can look at our life and discover that everything in it is a reflection of some aspect of ourselves. Something within ourselves similar to current outer situations attracted almost every aspect of those outer life experiences. For this to be true, it becomes immediately apparent that this law does not operate merely on superficial levels. Our lives are usually filled with a wide range of people and situations, some appearing very different from how we perceive ourselves. In order to understand the operation of "Like attracts like," we have to recognize that not only are the conscious levels of our minds reflected in our experience but the subconscious levels as well.

RUTH—UNKNOWN FEELINGS MANIFEST

Ruth had tried very hard to communicate clearly with her mother-in-law, whom she dearly loved and respected. One day she suddenly found herself the object of an angry tirade launched by her mother-in-law. In trying to understand what had happened, she asked a teacher who understood the Universal Laws why this event had occurred. She was aware of the Law of Begetting through which we experience what we have done to another. She could honestly say that she had not expressed anger and hostility like that to others.

The teacher explained to her that there is another part of the Law of Begetting, the Law of Attraction, and that it operates to draw to us emotions and situations that reflect what we are holding within. It was not enough not to express anger. If she were holding anger within herself, she would draw expressions of anger into her world. As she honestly examined her own feelings, Ruth recognized that she was carrying very deep anger that related to her mother-in-law and mother figures in general. She began to work on the healing of her anger.

CHANGING OUR CREATION

The thoughts, feelings, beliefs, and attitudes we hold in our minds and hearts create our life situations through the Law of Attraction and the actions we express outward through the Law of Begetting. It is easy to see that the way to change our lives is to change those thoughts and feelings. While it may be easy to come to that conclusion, to actually make that change is not as easy. I have tried diligently to control the thoughts in my mind and change some of my deeply held beliefs. Unfortunately, they change when I focus my mind upon them and revert back to prior form when my attention wavers, which it usually does in a minute or two.

Imagine for a moment that you are an automobile builder and have built a car that you are now selling. You have found that many of the ideas you had used in building this car were not structurally sound and that some of the materials you used were defective. Wouldn't you naturally want to build a new, better car that incorporated the more advanced concepts and superior materials that you were discovering? The same is true of us as we learn more about how we build our life experiences. We have the natural desire to be more effective at creating a life that expresses our inner capabilities.

As a result of the Laws of Cause and Effect, we meet each aspect of what we have created by attracting the effects of our thoughts, feelings, beliefs, and actions into our life so that we can learn from that situation, find a higher response, and express the creative power of our response. With each response we have to our old creation, we have the opportunity to bring forth a greater creation. These give us the opportunity every moment to rebuild what we have created.

The Laws of Cause and Effect are a very wise system in terms of learning about our creative power. But what if we have made the same mistake sixteen times? Do we really have to live through all sixteen times of that mistake repeating even if we can learn the lesson in less? Do we have to face every fear we have in order to change our belief structure? A car manufacturer throws away old forms and molds when a new one is created. Sometimes he designs a new car rather than simply redoing the old one. Using the Laws of Cause and Effect to change our lives can appear like trying to build a new car by replacing every bolt in the old one as it breaks and every piece of material as we become aware of its defect. As we slowly rebuild it, we end up with new material in the same old car.

Fortunately, the wisdom that ordained the Universal Laws of consciousness created a way for us not only to learn from our errors but also to design a new car and move on to an airplane. The system of laws that provides the opportunity to make major changes in our creative pattern are the Laws of Transformation.

Let's begin our examination of the Laws of Transformation with two experiences—one the dramatic change that demonstrates clearly the power of another order of law at work, and the other an ordinary, everyday kind of transformation, the kind that really determines the quality of the minute-by-minute experiences of our lives. Both involve a change brought about by the operation of the Laws of Transformation.

MARTHA

Martha was plagued by constant fatigue. It took a major effort for her to accomplish anything. In addition to this, she had a nerve disease which brought continual discomfort. Through diet and exercise, she was able to control the effects of these problems to a point where she could function at a minimal level, but she longed for the experience of energy and good health. Martha tried to meet her situation by maintaining a positive, confident attitude, but the difficulties seemed endless.

Martha had done much reading, studying, and reflection to try to understand her situation and discover ways of helping herself. As a result of her sincere desire she had a profound inner experience. One evening instead of being tired, she found herself in a strange state of wakefulness, very calm and relaxed. She began to review events from her life as though guided by what she called a ".Jesus-like presence." She not only felt loved, but also experienced sincere love for those in her life. After the experience, Martha was filled with energy. She went out and shared her experience with her friends, with energy remaining to share with her family that evening. She discovered that she was cured—instead of disease, she had health, energy, a sense of purpose, and a whole new joy and zest for living.

Many people have met problems similar to Martha's by supporting their healing through gradually changing their thought patterns, understanding their emotional reactions, and choosing different responses. Realizing that how we think, feel, and act creates our life experiences through the Laws of Cause and Effect, these people have used these laws to bring about the gradual improvement of their health by facing their old perceptions and changing them day by day, experience by experience. What happened for Martha was different. One day the problem was there, the next day it was gone. What was the difference between her experience and the others'? The difference was that Martha experienced the Laws of Transformation. There were still parts of her old creation she had to face, but she met them from a new position that included the health and energy which her old creation had denied her.

Cases of rapid transformation from unhealthy situations to healthy ones in which emotional, mental, and even physical limitations appear to be set aside are often the result of the Laws of Transformation at work. In the following chapters we will examine many people's experiences as we explore these remarkable laws which seem to virtually change the past and bring forth a new present and a new future.

While it is helpful to realize that the Laws of Transformation make dramatic instantaneous changes like Martha's possible, most of our needs for the assistance of the transformative laws are more mundane, but no less important. It is the moment by moment experiences, how we respond to the series of little events in our days, that the scientists are saying can have the greatest impact on our well-being. Medical, psychological, and stress researchers are telling us it is the accumulation of our responses to the little stressful events, one after another, that is behind seventy-five percent of our doctor visits. This is called chronic stress, and it is debilitating to our bodies, minds, and spirits.

It is the tension of having to get the children off to school when you can't find their shoes, being late for work, the traffic jam on the freeway, finding the eighty-seven e-mails on your computer when you sit down, and having to attend the urgent meeting that disrupts an already overdue project. These are not big experiences; they are normal, everyday happenings. They are, however, the paper cuts that accumulate and drain energy, meaning, quality, pleasure, and health from our experience. It is here that the application of the Laws of Transformation is the most important.

WOMAN AT THE BRIDGE

I live in mountain country. The back road that connects my home to the main highway follows a river for about a mile, crosses a one-lane bridge, and then rises to the highway. One day I was very late to work. I drove the narrow road faster than usual and arrived at the one-lane bridge. My wife was right behind me in her car.

A car was coming down the hill toward the bridge, but I was on the bridge and three quarters of the way across before the other car, an old VW bus, arrived at the other end of the one-lane bridge. My wife pulled onto the bridge following me across. The VW bus did not pull over to wait for us to get off the bridge; instead it pulled right in front of the bridge and stopped. There was no way off of the bridge with it sitting there. We had stopped our cars to avoid hitting the vehicle and waited for the woman who was driving to back up. She simply sat there. It took me a few moments to comprehend that she was not going to let us off the bridge. I thought of getting out and talking to her (I hope I would have talked!), but I did not have the time to negotiate for an exit from the bridge. I motioned for my wife to back up, and the two of us backed our cars across the bridge and onto the road. The woman proceeded to cross the bridge and drive past us, after which we were free to continue on to work.

As I pulled away, I felt the anger and frustration of the ridiculous experience I had just had. The truth is, it cost us about two minutes of time and was insignificant to my day. However, my mind would not let it alone. I analyzed it in different ways, coming up with the words I should have said to the woman.

I know that my thoughts and attitudes have a profound effect on my life. I told myself not to keep thinking about it. However, as you have probably experienced, the thoughts continued with all the feelings of frustration and irritation originally felt, triggering the physical stress responses of such thoughts. While the stressful thoughts were taking place, the hormones being dumped into my system were literally accelerating my aging process and reducing my capacity for clear thinking. Fortunately, there are techniques for utilizing the Laws of Transformation which allow us to make changes in our system that release us from the tyranny of our repetitive thought patterns.

When I utilized the techniques that gave me access to the Laws of Transformation, I suddenly looked up and realized it was an absolutely beautiful morning. I was driving through a redwood forest and the patterns of light coming through the trees were exquisitely beautiful. I felt the joy of a beautiful morning and the release and freedom from the tyranny of my own thoughts and emotional reaction.

This is a simple use of the Laws of Transformation. However, that change—the transformation in a moment from stress and frustration to serenity, beauty, and clarity—is neither a small nor insignificant accomplishment. The moments of our lives determine the quality and fulfillment we experience. To be able to transform the moment is a goal that has been the focus of religion, philosophers, and wise beings for ages. It is through the Laws of Transformation that we accomplish this change.

The remainder of this book will focus primarily on the Laws of Transformation such as the Law of Love (chapter 3), the Law of Giving (chapter 6), the Law of Forgiveness (chapter 7), the Master Law of Relationships (chapter 9), the Law of Faith (chapter 10), the Laws of Mercy and Balance (chapter 11). However, I will also discuss other key Universal Laws such as the Law of Wisdom (chapter 8), the Law of One (chapter 12), and the Law of Grace (chapter 13). To help readers further understand the Universal Laws and how to apply the important transformative Law of Love, I have included chapters on attunement (chapter 4) and how to love (chapter 5).

In the next chapter I want to offer you some of my personal experiences in exploring and learning the laws, which I hope will explain some of the important dynamics of the Universal Laws. I will also introduce you to the work of Doc Lew Childre whose ideas have helped me truly understand why the Laws of Transformation can work so powerfully in an individual's life.

Chapter 2

Discovering Dimensions
of the Law

A PERSONAL JOURNEY

My journey of personal discovery is not greatly different from anyone else's, anymore than if we took separate trips across the continent. They might involve different routes, towns, and scenery. But in essence, our journeys would be of traveling through the plains and mountains, as well as meeting the people of the land. My journey has led again and again to the exploration of the laws, and to an understanding that has grown and changed with each experience. Along this journey I have challenged the laws, worked with them, disavowed them, and taught them. At this point in my journey, I offer to you a statement of those laws as I understand them now with many details of this journey interspersed in the chapters that deal with the specific laws.

A CHILD'S PERCEPTION

Most of us have had moments in childhood when we touched that divine presence. We did not think it extraordinary because it wasn't; it was just a beautiful moment filled with love. In those simple moments our hearts were alive, and we saw the poignant beauty of life vividly with wonder and appreciation.

I recall one such moment. I was about twelve years old, filling a bucket of water while feeding my horse and enjoying my work. The fullness of my heart is not possible to describe, yet it was simple, not cosmic, nor an altered state in any sense. It was

13

more like being fully, joyfully, completely present in the midst of divine love at work.

Remembering back to that moment, I realize that I felt not only the love but also the order of the laws. I had a subconscious awareness that this order sustained my life and worked for me with love. Of course that was not part of my childhood understanding. The awareness of the law that I had then was only a feeling that I can now recall, an understanding barely under the surface of that heart-filled moment. Many years later at a conference in the Cayce headquarters in Virginia, I listened to Everett Irion, one of the outstanding interpreters of Cayce's wisdom. He described the order that Edgar Cayce had attributed to the Universal Laws, and I connected with that same feeling, the power of divine love working to teach me, mature me, and care for me.

That conference took place in my college years. As I went forward in my life, I tried to learn about those laws, to test them. The concepts challenged the world I saw. The world appeared filled with good and bad, have and have not, injustice and the need for a great struggle to bring order and fairness. I entered law school to participate in that struggle.

LOSS AND PAIN

Before my graduation came my first and greatest test. My wife and I had been part of a meditation group and involved in family and raising our baby daughter, Lisa. I was preparing to graduate from law school, and she was substitute teaching until she received a permanent teaching position. Life was good and full and beautiful. Then in one day that was gone. Her life was ended by a man with a gun, and I was in loss, grief, and deep confusion as I looked at life through pain.

The concepts that spoke of God as omnipresent and all good seemed hollow and empty of meaning or validity. Yet as I looked at my life and the pain I felt for myself, my little daughter, and our families, something inside me required that I reach for another understanding of my reality; that I not let my pain be my only truth. I understand now that in my sincere inner asking I invoked the great Law of Wisdom (see chapter 8). At the time, it was only a desire to know the truth. A part of that desire was to forgive if I could; but the most important part was to focus on the love my wife and I had shared and on my love for my daughter. I was not to surrender those to my anger and pain.

A NEW PERCEPTION

Some of the understandings I sought came quickly, others some years later. About two months after her death, I experienced a change in my perception that became the ground floor from which I could build a new understanding of those events and of life.

I had gotten up from the floor where I had been playing with Lisa who had just had her first birthday. I sat in the chair and looked at her, wishing she could still have present in her life the great love and care that her mother had felt for her. I suddenly noticed that she continued to play as though there were someone there with her. She reached out as though responding to another person and then pulled back and laughed as though she were being touched. For fifteen or twenty minutes as I watched with a sense of incredulous joy, she went on playing as I had often seen her do with her mother. I knew she was having a moment when her mother was able to reach through the doors of ordinary sense perception and be fully there with her in a special reality open to her yet invisible to me.

Then I experienced a wave of love sweep over me. It was so deep and all encompassing that years later as I write of it, I can still feel it in my body and its touch upon my spirit. It was the experience of pure love — personal and way beyond the personal. I knew I was loved, completely, unconditionally, and eternally. I knew that was the true reality of being, mine and everyone else's. It was not reasoned; it was experienced, it was known.

Today, I understand some of that shift of awareness. A new perception of life was opened to me through the stimulation of my heart from my love for my daughter and the response of the amazing power of divine love. I dwelt for a moment in another dimension of reality where the duality of our world is not the truth, but the presence of infinite love and wisdom is the true reality of life. It was not a dimension separate from my world and life experiences, but rather one I had not yet learned how to access. Yet it had opened because my asking and caring had set the Laws of Transformation in motion.

I understood that the tragic events that had filled our lives were a part of another creation that I was not seeing fully but whose goodness I now felt and knew to be present. Over the

months that followed, many new perceptions and understandings came to me from within and without. I learned of the events
of my wife's death from another spiritual perspective. I came to
see that experience and my life differently—as events that were
the result of great love and care set in motion to accomplish a
purpose to which we had all agreed. The result was a very personal look at the Universal Laws which I had used to create my
life experience. An additional result was the expanding experience of great love, care, learning, and facilitation in my life, as I
consciously sought to live in accordance with the purpose of
those laws.

Some years later, another part of the asking of that early moment with Lisa was fulfilled. A wonderful woman, who brought
not only love for me but deep love for Lisa as well, came into our
lives. For many years she has been my wife and Lisa's mother. I
was blessed to watch the fulfillment of that early prayer for my
daughter come into expression at all levels.

It would be inaccurate to say that the experience of death left
no pain. Years later as Lisa and I talked, I came to understand
that the loss of her mother took away a happiness from her that
was never replaced. She has gone on to a life of great meaning,
that includes its own happiness. Yet that loss has remained. For
me, the perspective of good and bad was released as a higher
perspective was sought. In that seeking 99 percent of my pain
was healed and my reality became that of the love that underlies
all of our creations. And the one percent? It remains a gentle
poignancy in my life.

LEGAL CAREER

As an attorney, I participated in that struggle to make life
better. I spent six years practicing man's law, most of that time
as an assistant attorney general in New Mexico, helping to bring
environmental solutions to the deteriorating air quality in that
beautiful state and attempting to stop the extensive land fraud
that was trashing a fragile ecology and stealing the savings of
people from all over the country. These were effective years in
the third-dimensional (outer-oriented) perspective. My activity
varied from the United States Supreme Court, to the top of the
smoke stacks at the huge four corners generating plant, to many
meetings with people rich and poor who bore the cost of our
acute lack of care for each other in our society. I saw the costs of

living in a very narrow three-dimensional perspective of life—win, lose, right, wrong, my rights . . . I came to appreciate that all the spiritual wisdom I heard and studied over those years is of no earthly good, if it doesn't make a real change in people's lives, clear down to the physical level.

I had the chance to watch the Universal Laws work in many situations. As I honestly looked at them and assessed my life, I realized that I was at the effect end of life instead of the cause end. The changes I was able to achieve in our man-made legal system were the results of people reaching for a greater harmony within themselves. Changes happened from people listening to their own hearts instead of just a paycheck or a political or power-motivated perspective. I realized the only real answer for our external environment depended upon a change in our internal environment. Not only did I have my experiences during those years to teach me those things, I received a view from another perspective.

THE LAWS OVER TIME

I spent about six weeks doing some inner work to lessen my allergies. I knew there were emotional links to the allergies so I began the investigation of those emotions. Without any outer stimulation other than a friend asking me to look deeper, the memories of many lives spent in the earth had opened before me. In most I recalled being a victim of war, disease, slavery, violence, starvation, and abuse. Then I explored why I had suffered so greatly and discovered that in my early experiences in the earth I used the personal power I had to spread human misery in all those forms. When I looked for solutions to end that cycle, I discovered lives in which people had begun to share with me the experiences of giving and caring. I began to take a small part in helping others. My role as a victim started to end and meaningful purpose began.

I saw the laws work. I discovered that life was in the long run just and fair, that we meet ourselves in life, and that changing our lives depended upon changing ourselves. This was the plan of the Universal Laws: to allow us as cocreators to learn the nature of our creations and to offer us harmony with the higher purpose of life through the doorway of the care and love within our hearts.

From these experiences, inner memories, and observations, I

explored the meaning of my role in the world and decided to reach for a way of transformation. Kicking and complaining, I entered the ministry.

MINISTRY, LABORATORY FOR THE LAWS

In ministry in the Unity Church the real learning began. I had a large group of people who shared their lives with me. They were working with the Universal Laws as they understood them, and I assisted them with my understanding. I was privileged to watch their lives unfold as they applied the laws. Sometimes the laws worked as I expected; sometimes I could not understand the results and would have to explore deeper. In this exploration, my father, Bruce, who had also been fascinated by Cayce's statement of the Universal Laws, joined me. He and my mother researched the laws and Cayce's readings on the laws in depth, while my study focused on exploring different spiritual systems and behavioral patterns. All of the world's religions acknowledged the laws, but their teachings were for the most part particular applications rather than statements of the laws themselves.

It was in ministry that I discovered the dimensional nature of the laws, the ordered levels at which the laws worked. I would watch as people dealing with a problem applied a law to their lives. They would love, forgive, pray, ask, affirm, seek positive thoughts, give, or assist others. As I watched, two differences became readily apparent. The first was that the use of some laws brought greater change and more rapid change than others. These I came to realize were the Laws of Transformation. They moved the person from a place in creation where he or she was stuck, to a totally new experience. The slower laws were the Laws of Cause and Effect. They demonstrated a more linear relationship between the cause of change and the effect that was experienced. The Laws of Cause and Effect, while they brought change, took a much longer time to fully manifest that change.

DIMENSIONS AND THE LAWS

Even within the transformative laws some applications brought stronger, faster results than others. Bruce and I, seeking an understanding of this dynamic, found ourselves at the Institute of HeartMath, where we consulted the wisdom of Doc

Lew Childre, its founder. It was from Childre that we got the key to this difference in transformative energy. The major difference is that the Laws of Transformation connect us to higher dimensional energy levels.

A concept of dimensions is helpful to the understanding of why the Laws of Transformation work at a different level and effectiveness than other laws such as the Laws of Cause and Effect. It also explains some of my experiences with the laws that led me to this work. For those reasons I will digress for a moment to share a simple concept of dimensional energy and intelligence with you.

A NOTE ON UNDERSTANDING DIMENSIONS:

The Law of Love (chapter 3) is the primary law of transformation. The Law of Love is "Love transforms" and when one sincerely loves from the heart, transformation takes place at many levels of a person's being as we will explore in the next chapter. By learning a little more about the levels of divine intelligence (dimensions) that the Law of Love provides us, we bring its operation out of the realm of mystery and into the world of ordered functioning to which the laws belong. Love felt deep within the heart is the access code to higher dimensions of energy and intelligence. When we are talking about dimensions, we are simply describing ordered levels of intelligence that are available to all of us.

THIRD DIMENSION

We are all familiar with third-dimensional existence. This is where the third-dimensional or physical aspects of life are our predominant reality—the physical necessities like food, shelter, and the pleasures and fears associated with the physical world. Love and care exist in important ways in the third dimension. They include providing the physical necessities of life and the experience of the wonderful pleasures of our material world. Most of humanity lives in this reality. When people are focused upon third-dimensional reality, their perceptions are very dualistic—good and bad, right and wrong, winner and loser.

This dimension provides a wonderful bottom-line test of our spirituality: Does it bring transformation into this physical level of experience? Does it result in our living more effective, meaningful lives? Does our spirituality help us care for our families, our neighbors, and manifest our individual purposes in concrete ways?

LOWER FOURTH DIMENSION

The fourth-dimensional levels of intelligence can be looked at in three basic aspects — lower, middle, and higher fourth-dimensional intelligence. In the lower fourth-dimensional experience, the individual becomes aware that there are other aspects of life as important as his or her own physical concerns. Here the social conscience awakens — contribution to others, concerns for the hungry, the environment, community, and planetary well-being. Individuals awaken to the awareness that we are not separate but interdependent and bear a responsibility beyond ourselves to the whole.

However, the concerns of the third dimension are not excluded. In fact each higher-dimensional level includes those preceding it. What changes at each higher level is one's understanding and way of perceiving life that in turn changes what has primary meaning, value, and importance to the individual. A different nature of intelligence is guiding the choices, understandings, and perceptions of life at each level.

MIDDLE FOURTH

At the middle fourth dimension we find the understanding that it is from within that we create our world. Much of our work in learning to accept ourselves and to apply the Laws of Cause and Effect that operate primarily from the mind occur at this level. Many religious experiences and teachings are found here. At this level rituals and processes invite us to work upon ourselves and to change ourselves and thus our world from within. Much of psychological processing is utilization of middle fourth-dimensional intelligence. This is a very important level because we take responsibility for our creation and actively focus on our inner life where we can release our blocks and discover our greater creative powers. Psychic phenomena and the study of what is beyond the physical, including ancient knowledge, are found in this dimensional energy as well.

There is a difficulty with the middle fourth-dimensional energy. It involves a lot of process and very little of it manifests into the third-dimensional world. We find ourselves forever working it out, processing it, getting in touch with it, praying about it. We do change our relationship to whatever it is, but that change does not always bring great changes in our lives. Breakthroughs bring us demonstrations but not substantive shifts in real time that are sustainable. This is not the fault of anything that is done at this level. This is the way the energy is structured at the middle fourth dimension. This energy does not easily penetrate the density of the third dimension. Therefore it takes a lot of work over time to bring the changes into manifestation and often we seem to go one step forward and two steps back.

UPPER FOURTH

The upper fourth-dimensional energy is very different. It easily and directly penetrates and relates to the third dimension. It is fast, incisive, and without a great deal of process. Because it penetrates the third dimension, its intelligence is very effective in bringing our values and ideals into manifestation. It is strong in its purpose, and when we follow its intelligence we bring manifestation to our purpose. It brings our experience of God or divine presence into a living, active, applied experience rather than merely contemplation. It is powerful and effective.

The experience of love that the higher fourth dimension brings has warmth and care, but it is not coddling. Rather it is transforming. Instead of processing, it transforms. Dwelling in the middle fourth energy tends to make one spacy, floaty, and often we find it difficult to relate to the world. Dwelling in the higher fourth-dimensional energy makes one grounded, energized, ready to meet life. It is what Jesus talked about when He said, "I am in the world but not of it." If He had been speaking of middle fourth-dimensional energy, He would have probably said, "I am not in the world and wish I weren't of it."

Higher fourth-dimensional intelligence sees the broader perspective and gives practical steps to bring solution and effective change. It is often very directive and the term we might most often associate with it is "common sense." In my experiences with the middle fourth intelligence, the guidance I would often get was "patience," "have faith." The guidance I receive from the higher fourth dimension is "do this," "try this," "this way of approaching it would be more effective." Jesus demonstrated higher fourth- and fifth-dimensional energy. He did not have people enter into process of self-discovery and analysis to heal. He said "heal" and it was done.

FIFTH DIMENSION

When we understand fifth-dimensional intelligence, it is easier to conceptualize the higher fourth energy. In the fifth-dimensional intelligence, efficient use of energy is its criteria. It manifests divine purpose without nurturing the egos involved. The biblical phrase for this energy was "God is no respecter of persons." There is no "working things out" with fifth-dimensional intelligence. The things are simply done. An example of fifth-dimensional energy entering the earth was the fall of the Berlin Wall and the collapse of the Soviet Union. There was no planning those things. No one expected them to happen. There was not a process of change. There was a change of frequency. The frequencies in mass consciousness that would support those things were withdrawn, not because they were good or bad, but because they were no longer efficient to a critical mass of people or to divine purpose.

One of the reasons people in all walks of life, all around the world are feeling life speeding up and experiencing very rapid change is that more higher fourth- and fifth-dimensional energy is entering the earth. The result of this change is that we need the heightened efficiency of the higher fourth-dimensional intelligence to successfully meet those changes. When we do not access those energy levels, we experience the stress of being out of harmony with divine purpose. We find a buildup of stress in our world and in our bodies.

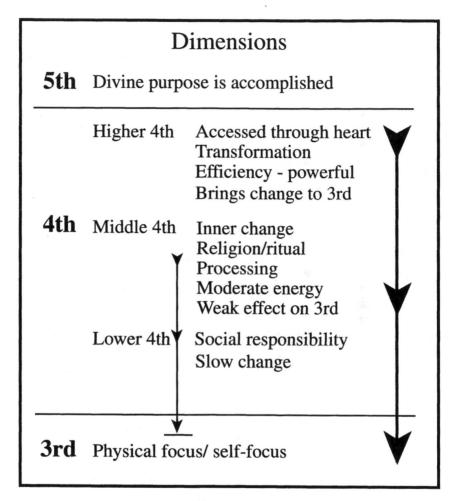

Figure 2A

ACCESS CODE

In the computer world, we often use access codes, a specific number or phrase, to be able to use a part of the computer system. If you know the access code, you can get the information that is there, if you do not you can't get to it. The access code to the higher fourth-dimensional intelligence is love. It is the bottom-line frequency of the higher fourth and fifth dimensions. The Law of Love is our key to bring that transformative power into our lives. Love is the access code for each individual and for humanity. Humankind has thousands of years and many great teachers who can help us transform our world to one based on a sincere love consciousness and intelligence. The processing time to accomplish that transformation is running out. It is time to do it. Only through love can that happen. The key to love is the human heart. The heart is where the spiritual intelligence of the higher dimensions enters the human system.

As we explore the Law of Love and the other transformative laws again and again, we will be brought back to the heart as the point of invocation of the laws. You will read about processes and techniques that have more middle fourth energy (more processing) in them and also simpler, more effective techniques that make a direct connection to the core frequencies of the heart, thus accessing higher fourth-dimensional intelligence.

These differences are not better or worse. At different times, different techniques will be more attractive for you to use in transforming your experience. If you want to go to Chicago, you can use freeways or use the two-lane roads. They are different journeys, and you will perceive different things along the way. Sometimes you want to get there right away. Sometimes the journey is as important as the destination. Most of the time, you will end up in Chicago. Sometimes you can get lost on the back roads, but either way you can have a meaningful journey. The more directly your inner work brings you into the experience of love, the more you are invoking the Law of Love and the transformation will be more direct.

DIMENSIONS IN MY PERSONAL EXPERIENCE

Much of the work I had done with the Universal Laws occurred within the middle fourth-dimensional energy structure. A group of us working together on these laws would pray for a solution, affirm a change we believed to exist at a spiritual level, and work diligently to bring the new creation into manifest form, whether it was healing, money, understanding, harmony in a group, peace of mind, guidance, or a new job for someone. These things would manifest as we applied the different laws. Many of them, while creating some constructive change in the individual's life, did not produce the full transformation I knew was possible. However, in the midst of many such experiences there would come one in which a change would occur that was deep and profound, quick and effective. We seemed to be applying the same laws, so what was the difference?

From Doc Lew Childre's writings and instruction, I came to understand that the relationship between the head and the heart influenced the law. In those cases where the transformation was slower, the mind kept a hold on the process. Love was involved, so the heart energy that was necessary for the transformation to take place was there and results were achieved. However, they were slow and sometimes incomplete. When we mix the head and heart like cochairs running a committee, there is a limitation on the amount of energy that can flow though the heart. So the change is not as fully and completely manifest.

The middle fourth-dimensional energy is a blend of the third-dimensional energy where we hold our dualistic head perceptions and the higher fourth- or pure fourth-dimensional intelligence where there is no dualism. Many of the Laws of Cause and Effect, which can be used to bring very constructive change in a person's life, operate at this middle fourth-dimensional level. That is why they do not produce the same kind of change that is found in the Laws of Transformation which work with the higher fourth-dimensional energy.

In the higher fourth perspective, Spirit takes us through the experience of different feeling, thoughts, and experiences as we learn about our creative abilities. When one learning is accomplished and the understanding gained, we are on to the next and the more limited form is released. When there is true surrender to the heart, as with the Laws of Transformation, we move out of the committee system and tell our higher self to run the show. At this point the head changes its role to become an effective translator and interpreter. It then assists us in bringing the higher intelligence into linear comprehension. This is very efficient and fully uses the love in our hearts as the full transformative energy. The bridge from the middle fourth- to the higher fourth-energy levels is through the deeper love in the heart.

When I experienced the increased efficiency of the heart intelligence and power compared to the mind work, I realized how beneficial this could be for all people. Having served as a minister, I realized this higher fourth-dimensional intelligence was the key tool for clergy who were trying to support people in their growth. If they and the people in their churches could grasp the difference effective use of the heart could make, they would be able to bring about rapid, meaningful transformation into their lives. It was this vision that became a part of my guidance to leave church ministry and work as a minister to ministers through the Institute of HeartMath.

This change in our understanding of how the laws worked also served as the impetus for Bruce and me to complete this book on the transformative laws. Bruce recognized in the simplicity and directness of the new techniques developed by HeartMath (which operated directly with the heart feelings), a pure application of the transformative laws we had been studying for so many years. He saw that when people used these techniques that the higher fourth-dimensional intelligence provided them with guidance that directly impacted the third-dimensional reality in which they lived. People got answers that worked as well for business as for their spiritual lives. They transformed the emotional patterns that had crippled their effective living and responded to life with more wisdom, effectiveness, and joy.

A part of our examination of the Universal Laws revealed that the goodness of God's love was not confined to any belief system but was available to all people regardless of spiritual knowledge. To be truly universal, spiritual laws must work for the child as well as the priest, the businessman as well as the cab driver, the Hindu as well as the Jew, as well as the agnostic. The access code to the full utilization of these laws is the love we awaken within our own hearts.

The higher fourth-dimensional intelligence and power, which is accessed through the core heart feelings of love, forgiveness, care, appreciation, understanding, courage, etc., is the doorway to the highest application of the transformative power of the Universal Laws.

CINDERELLA

This description of transformation in terms of dimensional energy may or may not be new to you, but the movement to the heart for the transformative impact of the Law of Love is something we have been exposed to since childhood. Our folk tales give us illustrations through archetypal symbols of the movement from the head to the heart and the dimensionally different experience that results as our transformation occurs. Let's explore one of the best known fairy tales, the story of Cinderella.

While Cinderella is a young girl, her mother dies, her father dies, and she finds herself in a large beautiful house governed by her stepmother. The stepmother does not love Cinderella and sees her as fit only to do the most menial of jobs such as sweeping the cinders from the hearth, from which her name derives. Both of Cinderella's stepsisters are ugly and vain. They do not accept Cinderella as an equal but force her to wait upon them.

The story is our story—the journey of ourselves as souls who have entered the earth. We have lost our awareness of ourselves as children of God—the true mother/father symbol. We are being raised by false concepts that are not true about ourselves—the stepmother and stepsisters. They are our self-concepts. The stepmother symbolizes our lack of feeling lovable and of value, and the stepsisters our self-judgments of ugliness and inferiority. These concepts exist within our heads—the large house.

Even when we get a different idea, such as when the invitation to the ball arrives and we feel we should be included, the false concepts keep us from the true experience of the harmony and beauty promised by the ball. In the story the stepsisters and stepmother tear apart the dress Cinderella has made so she could attend the ball. At least Cinderella was a positive thinker and utilized what she had, but the story tells us that is not enough while the concepts of lack of love and inferiority are alive in our heads.

Cinderella then leaves the house and goes to the garden. It is in the garden that her transformation takes place. The garden is an ancient symbol of the human heart. She has made the journey from the head to the heart, and it is there she meets the fairy Godmother. The fairy Godmother is divine love—the deep care for us that we find in the heart. But that care is obviously at a different dimensional level. There is no making a dress—it appears with the touch of the wand as do the transformation of the pumpkin into a carriage and mice to horses. The fifth-dimensional transformative energy accessed through the heart doesn't process it; it does it. This is transformation. The heart contains the energy to make the changes in our lives. The self-concepts of ugliness and unworthiness are cut through, and we find the power to get us to the ball.

Of course we often slip back into our old self-concepts just as Cinderella returns to her rags and the cinders when the clock strikes twelve. But she has been to the palace, to that true house of consciousness where she is in the "kingdom of God"—in the presence of the king (God)—our true heritage and home.

The next step of our relationship to the heart is to bring it into operation in our lives in front of our old self-concepts, to make it the dominant consciousness even in the house (our heads). She does this by putting on the glass slipper—the symbol of clear understanding. Facing her head concepts of stepmother and stepsisters, she reaches for the clear understanding of the intuitive wisdom that is our heart intelligence. She is then transported out of the old house consciousness, where the head ruled, to the palace—the God-ruled awareness, the human heart. The prince lives there—the intelligence that is under the guidance of the Divine, the king.

You have glimpsed the promise of living in the palace in those moments when you felt life should be a ball instead of stress, work, and drudgery. You get to live in the palace of your own heart where you connect with God. That is the promise Cinderella offers to you, that through the love in your heart you really can experience deep transformation and live happily ever after.

Chapter 3

The Law of Love

To *live* love is to be love . . . for love is law, law is love.

(900-331)

THE LAW OF LOVE

"Love transforms."

The fundamental Law of Transformation, the law that allows us to bring transformation out of the world of spiritual rhetoric and into our lives—the law that brings heaven to earth—is the Law of Love. It sounds a little fluffy, not quite realistic, perhaps hokey and Pollyannaish. The truth is, it is tapping into the pure power that creates and sustains the universe, and there is nothing fluffy about it. There is tenderness, care, and a gentleness that is a deep part of the experience of this law. However, it is the gentleness of infinite power expressing care, as the parent for its child, not the softness of weakness. I invite you to explore this great law, its gentleness and its power—the Law of Love.

Transformation brought about through the Law of Love is primarily an internal experience. That experience changes how we feel, think, and perceive. The world we live in is changed because we are changed. Love does not only transform our mental/emotional nature, it also involves the physical system of our body which goes through profound changes as well.

When we love, we put the Law of Love into operation. However, love as a philosophical or intellectual concept does not bring about transformation. Many people have studied, talked, and thought about love without experiencing its transformative power. The law is not that the concept of love transforms; rather, the experience of love — the movement of love through our hearts — causes transformation.

THE LAW OF LOVE AT WORK

There are many different ways of experiencing love and each results in some level of transformation. When most of us think of loving, we initially conceptualize loving as expressing love or feeling love toward another person. The following two experiences are about loving others and the powerful transformative effect that that has. In the first experience the lawyer has made a commitment to change from his prior habitual responses and to choose to love when he enters into the normal interactions of law and family life. In the second, the teacher is simply performing her daily job responsibilities with the natural, sincere love she had for her students.

LAW OFFICE AND HOME

I have a friend who, when I met him, was a successful trial lawyer. He was tough and uncompromising and could chew up most witnesses with ease. As I came to know him, I discovered that early in his life he had been a practicing alcoholic which resulted in a divorce and estrangement from his children. My friend, now sober for many years, began working with the experience of love. He began to care about himself, and even though he was very worried it might ruin his business, he decided to try to bring love into his law practice.

He was amazed to find that his cases were much more successful and moved to resolution quicker because of the love he was bringing to his work. By caring about the people he was working with, clients, witnesses, or other attorneys, he found that he understood their perceptions better and was more effective at getting at the truth without the alienating effect of the verbal brutality that he had used in the past. His settlements were higher and his trials more effective. His office prospered. He also began to experience friendships with other attorneys whom he had thought hated him. However, the greatest result of his experience of loving was that his children, one by one, opened up to him. He established healthy, joyous relationships with each child. His joy at the return of his children to his life was a true delight to witness. He learned the amazing power of the Law of Love the only way we really can come to fully appreciate it—by living it.

I had a suspicion that bringing love into the law firm would be successful. I remembered researching the spiritual laws during my legal career and came across this amazing statement from Edgar Cayce. To a lawyer, he gave this advice about his law practice:

> . . . *to* those who are seeking such [legal] services that may be supplied, then that service—as love, as hope, as confidence, as courage—must be not only exhibited but manifested; and *the law works!* (877-19)

Cayce was not speaking of manmade law. He was encouraging this attorney to bring the Law of Love into his law practice. That is the law that works! When we go to a lawyer, are we not seeking transformation from some limitation or difficulty in our lives? It is through the Law of Love that transformation happens. That is the law that works.

Many years ago, I ran across this example of the power of the law of love applied in the slums. I was pleased to rediscover it recently in the book, *Chicken Soup for the Soul.*

THE POWER OF ONE PERSON'S LOVE

A college professor had his sociology class go into the Baltimore slums to get case histories of 200 young boys. They were asked to write an evaluation of each boy's future. In every case, the students wrote, "He hasn't got a chance." Twenty-five years later, another sociology professor came across the earlier study. He had his students follow up on the project to see what had happened to these boys. With the exception of 20 boys who had moved away or died, the students learned that 176 of the remaining 180 had achieved more than ordinary success as lawyers, doctors, and businessmen.

The professor was astounded and decided to pursue the matter further. Fortunately, all the men were in the area and he was able to ask each one, "How do you account for your success?" In each case the reply came with feeling, "There was a teacher . . . "

The teacher was still alive, so he sought her out and asked the old but still alert lady what magic formula she had used to pull these boys out of the slums into successful achievement.

The teacher's eyes sparkled and her lips broke into a gentle smile. "It's really very simple," she said. "I loved those boys."[1]

The transforming effect of love in our lives cannot be overestimated. It worked in the slums of Baltimore. It also works in your life, with your family, and with your friends.

From our study of the Universal Laws, we know that we each construct our world by the perceptions and patterns within us. The most effective application of the Law of Love is in the transformation of ourselves. As the patterns we hold are transformed, we are free to create our lives without those limiting patterns ruling our world. The following example is a very specific application of the Law of Love to a pattern within me that had plagued my life for many years.

CUT-THRU

I was at a conference where we had just completed the morning's agenda. We all headed for lunch, and I wondered with whom I would eat. The thought of approaching one of the other people produced a startling reaction in my body. I felt a visceral fear reaction, so strong that I had to fight with myself to walk toward the dining room. It made no logical sense. The people were a wonderful group, some of whom were friends and acquaintances of many years. However, the reaction was so strong that my body almost shook as I began to force it in that direction. I stopped and realized that something very serious was taking place. Attending to this need was far more important than lunch.

I went back to my room and began to bring the power of love to this intense reaction through a technique I had learned from heart science pioneer Doc Lew Childre. When I had practiced this technique called "Cut-Thru®"[2] on earlier occasions, I realized that I had finally come across a way of working with love that was so powerful that it could accomplish major transformation in a very short time. This fear reaction was so strong that it seemed a worthy test for Cut-Thru as a way of applying the Law of Love. (The technique is given in detail in chapter 9.)

The Law of Love is powerful and effective and always works to the extent that love is really applied. However, it's difficult to actually feel love in situations when our reactions are firing and filling us with strong emotions that dominate our responses and perceptions. When we are hurt, angry, or afraid, we do not feel like loving.

My fear reaction was extremely strong, and I remembered that it had often surfaced in social situations. My usual response was to suppress it so that I could function normally. This time I chose to apply the Law of Love. To do that, I first acknowledged and focused on the fearful thoughts and feelings that had suddenly surfaced. I then brought these feelings into the area of my heart to soak in the warmth of the heart energy. This effort reminded me of an experience I once had in a blizzard in Wyoming's Teton Mountains. Thoroughly chilled from being out in the severe snowstorm, I finally entered a warm lodge. Even though I knew the warmth of the lodge was there, what was most real was the intense cold I was feeling. Only after being in the warm lodge for a period of time did the chill begin to diminish.

Similarly at first, my feelings of fear seemed overwhelming, and I could hardly feel the warmth of my heart. As I continued to hold those feelings of fear in the area of my heart so that they could soak in the heart energy, the strength of the fear began to lessen. Gradually I became aware of the presence of love within my heart. As I continued to move through the steps of Cut-Thru, the feeling of love began to grow into a sense of love and compassion for myself. From that growing feeling of love, I began to experience strength, power, and security. The feeling of fear slowly dissolved.

One of the steps of Cut-Thru included feeling the original care that had somehow turned into this fear. Many reactions that we perceive as negative actually start out from an attempt to love ourselves or others by caring. I discovered that this original feeling of care was a type of self-love, a desire not to expose myself to situations that might result in rejection or hurt. That original impetus of caring for myself had become overcare, expressing as this irrational fear. Nothing in this social situation was any real threat to my well-being.

As I kept my focus on the feeling of that original love as care for myself, the transformation continued, releasing the old fear that had suddenly surfaced. I did not discover what incident had caused the pattern, where it had come from, any earlier experiences, or what it was all about other than the very general understanding that I just mentioned. Those types of understandings were not necessary. The strength of the love became so powerful that the feelings of vulnerability and fear were gone. It was transformed and has not returned.

In this situation, I had applied the Law of Love by using the steps of Cut-Thru which included bringing the feeling of fear into the heart area. It's rather like taking your cold to Dr. Love's office. Fortunately, Dr. Love also makes house calls.

MOTHER'S LOVE TRANSFORMS

Love's transformative power often touches us through another person's love. Just as Cayce was suggesting that the lawyer be an instrument of love in the lives of other people (the clients), so other people in our lives bring the energy of love to us. What is important is our receptivity to that love and the change it offers us.

The simplest experience of love and its transformative power is one almost all of us have had. As children, we would run to mother when we were hurt and climb up on her lap to be held and enfolded in her love. As we felt the security and power of her love encompass us, we began to relax, and the feelings of hurt, whether physical, mental, or emotional, began to dissolve, release, and disappear. In a few moments, the power of our mother's love had done its work, and we were running off to continue our adventures — happy and transformed from the momentary pain.

This simple image, the child being held by a loving parent, remains for me the most powerful expression of the Law of Love. It is what we are doing when we bring the expression of love into our lives. We are allowing the divine love to enfold us, move through us, and express as us.

MOTHER'S HEALING

Parents also get that love. I remember when my mother was visiting my daughter and me in Santa Fe, New Mexico. She became very ill on the evening of her arrival, and we discussed taking her to the hospital emergency room. She said she wanted to try to sleep that night and would reevaluate in the morning. The next morning she was up helping with breakfast, filled with energy and feeling wonderful. This was difficult to understand because she had been so very sick the night before. When I asked her, she told me of an experience she had during the night.

She had prayed for help with her illness and then tried to sleep. In a dreamlike experience, she saw a radiant figure surrounded by light. She recognized the figure as Mary, the mother of Jesus. The Blessed Mother was on a high hill, and people were coming to her. As they approached her, some as individuals, some as families helping a loved one, each was healed. My mother was there witnessing this event. Mary was in white and pale blue. She would touch a few, but for most people she looked at them—blessing them—and prayed. The healings came from within, a healing of love bringing changes at all levels and resulting in the expression of wholeness, peace, and serenity. My mother experienced being a part of it all—the light, the blessing, and the peace. Her own experience of sickness vanished, and she fell into a restful sleep knowing the illness was gone. She awoke filled with health and vitality.

In this experience, my mother felt and accepted the radiant love emanating from Mary. That love transformed her physical illness, eliminating all vestiges of it from her body. The transformation was immediate and complete. Love transforms.

Several of the above experiences involve the exchange of love—people being willing to express love to another and finding that love transformed their relationships, health, business, and self-perception. When we express that love, we are transformed, as was the lawyer. If others are receptive to that love, they are transformed, as were the children in the school, the child by the mother, the legal colleagues and family, and my mother.

Whether we study physics, psychology, or the spiritual laws, we end up concluding that the difficulties we face in our lives are the projections of patterns within ourselves into our world. For the experience of transformation to be effective, it must change those internal patterns. In the following experience, I was privileged to be a support as my friend consciously brought love to a limiting, internal pattern and allowed her love to transform that pattern. She did not have some of the simple techniques for applying love, such as Cut-Thru. However, she knew that within her were both the pattern and the love that could transform it. She made the internal journey to find the pattern and bring love to it.

VICTORIA

Her first reaction was rage; her second was tears. Victoria was deeply hurt by what this group of people, "the committee," had just told her. She knew their job was to evaluate her, yet she had thought of them as people who would be supportive of her as she neared the end of academic preparations for her new career. And why shouldn't they be supportive? She had done well in school; she was talented, innovative, intelligent, and personable.

The years of schooling were almost over, and now they told her they thought she was childish, too immature to handle the responsibilities of the new position for which she had been preparing herself. All of her positive attributes were of no avail. If there wasn't a change, she was out—rejected—blocked from her heart's desire.

Fortunately for Victoria, she understood the spiritual laws. Even though she wanted to deny what had been said ("I've already proven maturity and competence in my first career!"), she knew the committee could not reflect something about herself that was not there. The spiritual Law of Attraction, "like attracts like," which she knew to be unfailing, said it was her creation. With that awareness, she began the task of self-exploration. It was there she found little Vicki.

She found little Vicki by accepting the idea that she must be showing to others a childish self. She recalled the feelings she had when she felt insecure. They were just like what she had felt as a little girl when things were difficult at home. The more she remembered, the stronger the feelings became, until she could see the child in her mind and feel the fear that as a child had made her want to hide from the violence in her home. When she couldn't hide, she had tried to be cute and adorable so everyone would love her and she'd be safe. Victoria recognized that now, as an adult, this was a feeling that surfaced whenever she was afraid or insecure. She became that little girl acting through the adult. She tried to be lovable and pleasing, or to disappear and hide. She became little Vicki. This was what the committee had seen.

Victoria realized that much of her adult life was dependent on controlling the pattern of that little girl within her. She was an adult, a mother, a professional, but she was unable to hide little Vicki. She reflected on her own experience of motherhood. She recalled the way her daughter would at times be frightened until Victoria would hold her in her arms and give her total, unconditional love and understanding. As Victoria did this, her daughter's fears always subsided, and suddenly she would be ready to head back into life with the fear gone, feeling confident and expectant again. Victoria also remembered that whenever she tried to control her daughter, telling her not to act that way, not to feel that way, the girl would become angry and the situation would worsen.

With that same accepting, unconditional love, Victoria turned her attention to that inner part of herself that felt like a frightened child. She remembered what it was like to be that little girl as she saw and felt little Vicki's fears in her mind. As she experienced those painful memories, Victoria allowed the part of herself that was now an adult to feel caring and gentleness toward that immature part of her own being. As her feelings of love and compassion grew, she was able to reach out in her mind and hold out her arms to her inner child until the child could allow herself to be enfolded in Victoria's love.

I watched as Victoria imagined holding the child in her heart. The pain and tears that had been streaming down her face as she remembered the child's hurt and fear began to lessen. Gradually they faded as she assured her inner child over and over again, "I love you just the way you are." Finally, as little Vicki's hurts and fears eased, Victoria's face was filled with peace, and even a smile. She repeated this experience with the little girl inside herself a number of times over the next several days. When she next met with the committee, they remarked at the change in her expression of maturity and enthusiastically recommended her for certification in her new career.

Victoria discovered the Law of Love. The love she brought to little Vicki, who was a limited pattern of feeling and behavior from her past, healed the emotional hurts carried there for so many years. As love healed those hurts, they were transformed into that which is supportive of and in harmony with the rest of her being.

I first learned how to heal emotional wounds by applying love in the manner I had witnessed in Victoria's healing. In that experience she brought the love to her heart by remembering an

early experience of the feeling and then loving that part of herself that still carried that hurt self in her memory. This involved
looking into the past for causes of the pattern. It was not necessary to understand anything about that situation, simply
remembering the hurt and bringing the transforming power of
love to the hurt brought about the healing. At first it appeared to
me to be a very efficient method because long-held hurts healed
very quickly. However, there was a difficulty.

EASIER HOW TO'S

Because this way of applying the Law of Love involved remembering the past event and its emotions, it was very difficult for
someone to accomplish without another person facilitating the
experience and guiding one through it. Even with a skilled facilitator, people tended to get stuck in the story with its emotions
and perceptions. Without the facilitator, people who tried it usually got lost in the old feelings and often did not make the
movement into deep love.

Recently I learned from Doc Lew Childre several ways of accomplishing the same transformation without having to go back
into the original memory and feelings. The techniques, one of
which is Cut-Thru, which I mentioned above, are the easiest
ways to transform the deep emotional hurts that are stored in
our cellular memory. They work with the emotion at the level of
its energy or frequencies rather than with the memories attached
to it. The sharing of these highly efficient ways of applying the
Law of Love make it much easier for us to bring this transformative power into every aspect of our lives. These techniques are
described in chapter 5, "How to Love."

This transformative secret of love is no longer the exclusive
instrument of spiritual adepts or highly trained professional fa-
cilitators. It is because of their simplicity that these techniques,
developed by Childre, are being utilized to apply the Law of Love
in businesses, the military, families, classrooms, and all walks
of life. We've known about love since Jesus and other great spiritual teachers first instructed us to use it. Because of the simplicity
and effectiveness of these "how to's," we are able to apply our
knowledge of the Law of Love even in today's hectic lifestyle.

Love is an expression of the presence of God, Truth, or the
true spiritual nature. The teaching, "God is love," does not mean
God loves. It means God is the love that we experience. When we

encounter the divine presence, we recognize it through the set of feelings we have come to call love. Actually, those feelings are the response of our own human feeling nature to the presence of love, or God, moving within our hearts. As we allow that spiritual presence within us to flow into those areas where we hold limiting emotional or thought patterns, the limitations are transformed.

TRANSFORMATION IN THE PHYSICAL BODY

The above situations involved applying the Law of Love primarily to emotional hurts and their resulting perceptions. We looked at the example of my mother's healing where an effect was found on the physical body. Does our use of love regularly affect our physical bodies? The effect of positive mental and emotional states on the human system has been the focus of some groundbreaking research at Childre's Institute of HeartMath. This research gives us a look at the power of love to transform the physical body into a higher more efficient level of operation. Let's explore this process by examining the effect on the body of different feeling states.

HEART RATE VARIABILITY

Medical professionals have found that they can look at certain functions within our biological system to understand how well the body is operating. One function that is very important is heart rate variability (HRV) — the speeding up and slowing down of our heart rate. We all know that our heart beats at different rates, at times faster, at times slower. If we took our pulse rate while sitting and reading it might be an average of 65 beats per minute. If we took it after hiking up a hill, it might be an average of 120 beats per minute. This ability of the heart to change speed is part of what keeps us healthy. If we need more energy to go up the hill, the heart pumps faster; when we need less, as when reading, the heart knows to slow down. If we looked more closely at our heart rate, we would find that it changes not only when we change our level of exercise, but it also goes a little faster or a little slower with every beat. When we check our pulse to get a heart rate, we are getting an average rate.

By plotting those heart rate changes on a graph, a doctor can learn a lot about the health of several of our biological systems.

The graphs below are plots of heart rate variability. When the line is going up, heart rate is increasing; when it is going down, the heart rate is slowing down. A greater range between the high rate and low rate is good to see; it tells us our heart is healthy and can make changes quickly. Although the source of the heart beat is within the heart itself, it gets directions from the brain through the autonomic nervous system telling it whether to speed up or slow down. The part of the autonomic nervous system that tells it to speed up is called the sympathetic nervous system, and the part that balances that and tells the heart to slow down is called the parasympathetic nervous system. When doctors examine the heart rate variability pattern, they are learning about our autonomic nervous system as well. The heart rate variability graphs also gives us important information on how our body responds to the difference between feelings of frustration or stress and feelings of love such as sincere appreciation.

HEART RATE VARIABILITY—FRUSTRATION

Scientists discovered a dramatic demonstration of love's transforming power when they looked at the difference between

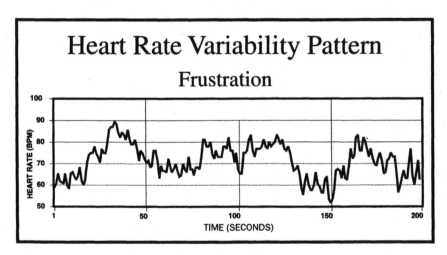

Figure 3A

Fig. 3A illustrates the heart rate variability pattern of a person feeling frustration which is characterized by its random, jerky pattern. This pattern is the result of imbalance in the autonomic nervous system.[3]

the effects of love and frustration on heart rate variability. If one is feeling frustration when the heart rate is being plotted, the following type of graph is produced.

With the feeling of frustration, the relationship between the increase and decrease of heart rate is a very chaotic one. What is actually happening is that the two branches of the autonomic nervous system are in conflict. One (the sympathetic nervous system) is trying to speed the heart up while the other (the para-sympathetic nervous system) is trying to slow it down. It is like driving a car with one foot on the brake and one on the gas. That would cause a lot of wear and tear on the engine and drive train, make the ride uncomfortable, and waste a lot of energy. The same is true of the heart. This pattern shows great inefficiency, stress, and waste of energy.

HEART RATE VARIABILITY—APPRECIATION

If we use sincere appreciation as an expression of a deep, heartfelt feeling giving expression to love, we see this picture of the change in the heart rate:

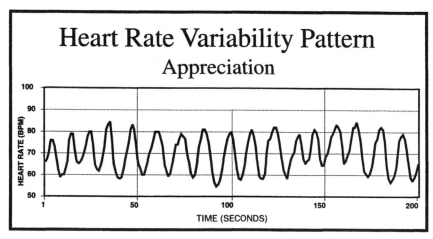

Figure 3B

Fig. 3B shows the heart rate variability pattern of a person feeling sincere appreciation. The ordered, balanced pattern is generally associated with efficient cardiovascular function. It is the result of the sympathetic and parasympathetic nervous systems working together efficiently.[4]

This shows the two functions of the autonomic nervous system working in balance with each other. This is a more youthful, efficient, harmonious utilization of the body's energy. It is a dynamic example of the transforming power of love operating at the level of our physical bodies. And yet it is only one of the many transformative effects of the Law of Love on human physiology. This balanced HRV pattern is the basis of another profound biological change. When this pattern is present in the heart, other systems in the body are strongly affected by its order and efficiency.

ENTRAINMENT

You have seen flocks of birds turn and move all together in perfect harmony; schools of fish do the same. That is an expression of a phenomenon called entrainment. One can observe entrainment occur in pendulum clocks which are oscillating at different rates but which over time come into sync with each other. Entrainment also occurs in the heartbeat of a mother and nursing baby as the baby's heartbeat pattern entrains to the pattern of the mother.

The heart is an oscillator just as a pendulum clock is an oscillator. With the clocks, the smaller pendulums entrain to the rhythm of the biggest oscillator. It is the same within the human body. We have many systems that are oscillators, and they entrain to the rhythm of the heart which is the body's biggest oscillator.

Here is a picture (fig. 3C) of three body systems: respiration, heart rate variability, and pulse transit time (blood pressure) when they are not entrained and then when they are brought into entrainment by utilizing a technique called FREEZE-FRAME®, which uses the transforming power of the love that flows through the human heart.[5] (Technique given in chapter 5.)

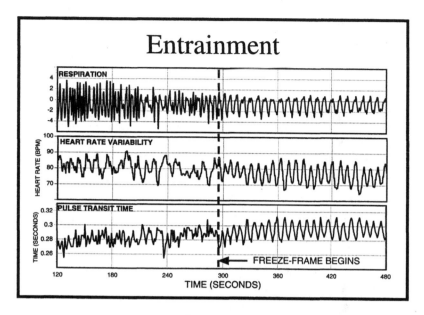

Figure 3C

Fig. 3C illustrates a phenomenon scientists call entrainment. Entrainment occurs when separate biological systems sync up with each other for highly efficient operation. In this graph, the parameters being measured are respiration, heart rate variability, and blood pressure (pulse transit time). Notice how the systems bear no relationship to each other on the left-hand side of the graph, but after the subject utilizes the technique FREEZE-FRAME, which is a specific application of sincere heartfelt feeling, such as love, the systems sync up and oscillate at the same rate. (The bottom graph is inverted, meaning higher time values equal lower blood pressure.)[6]

When this takes place, the body is operating at a new level of efficiency. This higher level of efficient operation saves energy and contributes to our having a greater feeling of energy and harmony. It is an example of the transforming power of love operating at the physical level of our experience. Love transforms us at every level. In later chapters we will explore other aspects of our physiological systems that are transformed through the Law of Love.

ROMANTIC LOVE

But will any kind of love produce this result? What about romantic love, one of the most universal forms of the love experience. It is easy to discount romantic love as being something other than the experience of the divine presence, but all love is the response within us to the Divine in our lives.

It is also true that there may be many other elements present in the romantic situation, including sexual excitement, enhanced self-esteem because of the attention from the other person, feelings of possession or security. Yet that which involves the unconditional acceptance of another person and beholds the value, the uniqueness, and the quality of that other person is the experience of the Divine. We become open to appreciate the precious worth, fine qualities, and beauty of that soul or spiritual being. We usually fall in love with those qualities which we perceive to be "godlike" in another person. When we fall in love, the feeling of love in the heart actually releases a greater level of intelligence into our system, and we are able to view others through a broader, more inclusive perspective. We see many unique and valuable aspects of their being that were closed to our perception before we came to love them.

EFFECT ON ANOTHER PERSON

How often has someone's love for us invited us to heal our limited perceptions and see ourselves as a being of value? One of the effects of the Law of Love is that our love supports others in loving themselves and thus in experiencing their own divine presence. But our love can only support. It cannot force another to open, heal, or experience the divine love which awaits even the slightest invitation to heal and transform. Each individual can also choose not to accept the transformative power of our love. They can remain as they are and not enter into the experience of transformation. When our love is freely given to those around us, it transforms not only our bodies and our worlds, but for those who are open, theirs as well.

ATTUNEMENT

The Laws of Transformation operate in part by bringing us into attunement with higher dimensional energy and intelligence. This process of attunement is activated by the Laws of Transformation, but also has its own laws as well. In the next chapter we explore the process of attunement to these greater aspects of our consciousness. With that understanding of attunement, we will then take another look at the Laws of Transformation and examine specific techniques that utilize this knowledge of attunement to activate the Law of Love in our lives even if we don't feel attuned—which is often when we need it most.

Chapter 4

Attunement

A human being is a part of the whole, called by us the "Universe," a part limited in time and space. He experiences himself, his thoughts, and feelings as something separated from the rest—a kind of optical delusion of his consciousness. This delusion is a kind of prison for us, restricting us to our personal desires and to affection for a few persons nearest to us. Our task must be to free ourselves from this prison by widening our circle of compassion to embrace all living creatures and the whole of nature in its beauty. Nobody is able to achieve this completely, but the striving for such achievement is in itself a part of the liberation and foundation for inner security.

Albert Einstein[1]

Through the Universal Laws, we can attune ourselves to higher levels of intelligence and wisdom, to our life purpose, and to ways of working in harmony with the people and situations in our lives. All Universal Laws involve attunement to some degree. To better understand the laws we will be exploring, especially the transformative power of the Law of Love, let's examine this important dynamic through which we literally attune to those forces that brought worlds into being. What is attunement? The dictionary defines *attune* as "to adjust, to bring into accord, harmony, or sympathetic relationship."

We attune ourselves every minute of the day, as we make our

choices to do this or that. By such choices we focus our minds and bodies on specific activities. In other words, we make an adjustment in our internal circuits to give our attention to some particular thing. That is a form of attunement. We all know how to attune ourselves to the outer activities of eating, dressing, driving a car, or watching television; most of these we do easily if not automatically. We also know how to attune ourselves to the more inner directed actions of sleeping or thinking. But how do we attune ourselves to our own spiritual nature?

FREQUENCIES AND VIBRATIONS

To learn more about attunement, let's consider for a moment the fundamentals involved in tuning a radio or T.V. set—a simple process of adjusting a dial to the desired station or channel. Technically it occurs because at that dial setting the circuits are tuned to, or receptive to, that particular frequency or vibration assigned for that station. The technical fundamentals of attunement are very clear. The basic frequency of a station is an oscillating wave which can actually be seen with proper equipment. A single cycle or vibration represents a flow of electrical current first in one direction and then in the other direction.

The number of such cycles per second is the frequency or rate of vibration. Each radio or TV station is assigned a particular frequency or vibration which it broadcasts. This is why you find it at a particular setting on your set. The program, music, or picture is superimposed on the basic vibration and is carried along with it.

THE RADIO TOWER

Many years ago when Bruce was an engineering student, he worked as a radio operator in a small broadcast station associated with the university which he attended. He tells of that time:

One of the summer jobs assigned to operators was to paint the radio tower. This very narrow, open, three-sided wood-frame tower, 300 feet high with cables strung to hold it vertical was a real thriller to climb. Suspended in the center of the tower from top to bottom was a power antenna, a heavy copper tube from which the broadcast signal radiated.

We would climb the tower and strap ourselves in to paint, always very careful not to touch the high-voltage antenna which hung only a foot or so away from us. We had learned the hard way that it could give us a severe burn, because it was operating while we were painting. We also learned, however, that we could hold a wrench in our hands, touch the antenna, and draw from it a beautiful electrical arc. We could even hear the program being broadcast in the sound of the arc. This was all very much against the rules, but then one does not learn unless one pushes the limits a bit. I have in my later years wondered why we were not killed by such shenanigans.

In any case, I became very much aware of the power in that antenna in the sky from which the signal radiated throughout the countryside. From my perch high above all, I could visualize the hundreds of people who had their radio sets attuned to our station's frequency, and who, through their sets were aware of the program being broadcast. I knew all this was taking place. Yet even though from my point in the sky I was at the very center of it all, I could not feel, hear, or see anything happening.

ELECTRICAL FORCES

It is quite a step from this to the realization that you and I, too, are broadcast stations radiating our signals to the world. We have a particular frequency or vibration—a consciousness or signal—which we radiate or broadcast. It is a composite of the particular frequency or vibration of our body, our mind, our heart, and our spirit. We are also receiving sets for we can attune ourselves to signals coming from within and without. Edgar Cayce's source tells us that we are electrical in nature.

Medical science is coming to greater realizations of this truth each passing year. Just as you attune your radio set to a station by adjusting its inner circuits, you can attune your body, heart, and mind to higher vibrations by adjusting your inner circuits. Recent studies show scientifically that we have different electrical waves in the brain and heart for different states of consciousness and that we can change these states. These processes, like all others, are governed by Universal Laws.

The readings make this startling statement:

Know then that the force in nature that is called electrical or electricity is that same force you worship as Creative
or God in action! (1299-1)AR

Another reading goes a step further and explains that the electrical forces within our bodies are indeed vibrations to which we
can attune, whether it be to a physical sense such as hearing or
to the spiritual force within us:

. . . life—God—in its essence is vibration, and—as the
physical beings are of that [same] atomic force . . . the
awareness of same, [God] is as to how conscious that vibration may be made . . . (281-4)

The reading goes on to explain that in the body, sight, hearing, taste, and speech are but different vibrations to which we
consciously attune and so become aware of them. We can likewise learn to attune to the higher vibrations, the essence of the
God force within us.

HEART FREQUENCIES

This attunement takes place by adjusting our own vibrations,
our own frequencies. We accomplish this through our thoughts
and feelings because thoughts and feelings are also expressions
of frequencies. As we stimulate these frequencies, we experience
them and associate them with specific thoughts or feelings. We
have the ability to select these frequencies, to choose our
thoughts and choose our feelings. These choices affect our receptivity just as the station to which we turn the radio knob
determines which radio frequencies we will receive. When we
turn our feelings and thoughts to those frequencies which are
close to or aligned with those of creative intelligence, we experience that intelligence.

How do we adjust our feelings to those of creative intelligence?
The clue is in the scriptural teaching that "God is love." (1 John
4:8 RSV) We experience that divine presence as the feelings of
love. When we are receptive to that frequency, we also receive
the intelligence or wisdom that is the expression of that love in
our lives.

How do we choose the love frequency, knowing that the moment when we often need that wisdom and love the most is when

we find ourselves in a situation in which love is the hardest to feel? Again the answer is vibrations. We select a specific feeling that resonates with the love frequency—one of the core feelings of the heart. Core heart feelings are certain feelings people have always recognized as deep expressions of the qualities associated with the heart. Such feelings include care, compassion, understanding, forgiveness, appreciation, courage, joy, and peace. We may not be able to choose the feeling of loving any time we want because of other emotions and perceptions that are active in our system; however, we can choose to experience one of the specific frequencies such as compassion, care, or appreciation. These activate the heart energy through which we feel the love vibration.

THE ELECTROMAGNETIC FIELD OF THE HEART

When we feel one of these core feelings related to love, we are stimulating the electromagnetic field that is generated by the beating of the heart.

Figure 4A is a diagram of the shape of the mathematical configuration of the electromagnetic field generated by your heart. Through this electromagnetic field we receive the love energy and its wisdom. This is the place where Spirit meets matter. Other systems within our bodies at various levels help to store, receive, and radiate those frequencies that carry the information from this unlimited source of intelligence.

JANE AND HEART INTELLIGENCE

The other day a young woman I'll call Jane approached me at a workshop I was conducting. She expressed her hopelessness at finding a way to relate to her husband in a particular situation that had developed in their relationship. She had tried to think of alternative ways of responding but had failed to come up with anything that seemed helpful. She did an exercise where she attuned herself to the greater wisdom that was accessible to her through the electromagnetic field of the heart. She did this by focusing on her heart and feeling one of those frequencies that are related to love.

At that moment, Jane could not feel love, but she could remember a joyful moment when she had played with her children. As she remembered and reexperienced that feeling, she was

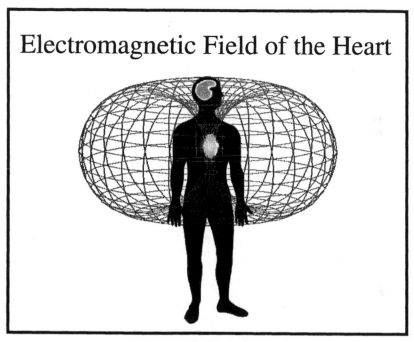

Figure 4A

Fig. 4A is a rendering of the mathematical model of the electromagnetic field that surrounds the human heart. It is subject to measurement up to twelve feet away from the subject. The diagram does not intend to imply that the head is not included because the waves go out in all directions. The diagram is indicative of the torus shape of the field.[2]

stimulating the electromagnetic field of her heart. She was dialing her receiver to the divine wisdom channel. Once that feeling was strong, Jane asked her heart what would be a more effective way to handle the situation with her husband.

She began to see his actions from a new perspective, and instead of seeing him as being critical of her, she realized that he was asking for recognition and validation. Jane said that would not be difficult for her to do, and she saw how she could also validate herself in that exchange. She had attuned to the higher wisdom within her heart which gives expression to the divine intelligence that was available to guide her life. In addition to the Law of Love, she had used the Master Law of Attunement to accomplish her connection with divine wisdom. Let's examine this Universal Law that is involved in our experiences of attunement.

THE MASTER LAW OF ATTUNEMENT

During the Great Depression, Cayce gave a reading for a Mr. Ames, one which was typical of hundreds given during those difficult years. The reading explained that fear prevailed in this country at that time because greed, avarice, and misunderstanding had taken away good judgment from many, and people struggled, not knowing why or for what. The source urged everyone, even those who were fearful, to come and open their hearts, their minds, and their souls to the law that has always been the answer to all such problems. It was the Master Law of Attunement.[3]

The Master Law of Attunement—"If you will be my people, I will be your God."

At the personal level, this is:

The Law of Divine Relationship—"If you will be mine, I will be your God."

This law is the covenant given through Moses to the Children of Israel.

And I will walk among you, and will be your God, and you shall be my people. Leviticus 26:12 (RSV)

In this simple statement lies the solution to your problems—to mine and to those of the world. But the first step is up to us. If we choose to turn to the Presence, the Creator of all, to attune ourselves to the source of life, then that Presence will be our source of all—all knowledge, all wisdom, all guidance, all abundance—because that is its nature.

Cayce's source insists that the divine forces are the only safe and sane power to depend on, that this law is the key to our relationship with the Divine, and that we ignore it at our peril:

Man has ever . . . when in distress, either mental, spiritual, or physical, sought to know his association, his connection, with the divine forces that brought the worlds into being. As these are sought, so does the promise hold true — or that given man from the beginning, "Will you be my children, I will be your God!" "You turn your face from me, my face is turned from you," and those things you have builded in your own endeavor to make manifest your own powers bring those certain destructions in the lives of individuals in the present . . . those [divine] powers that are so tabu by the worldly-wise, that are looked upon as old men's tales and women's fables; yet in the strength of such forces do *worlds* come into being! (3647-11)AR

If we choose to be His people, we accept and recognize that we are His children and that He will care for us, problems and all, no matter what the conditions around us may be. We rely on that divine power within us for guidance, rather than trying to use merely our own power or to depend on influencing others who seem to have the power in the world.

HEAD AND HEART

How does this attunement take place, and what does Cayce mean by specifying "your own power," as though that were a wrong or destructive thing? The easiest way to answer this riddle is to understand the relationship between the head and the heart. Our intellect and the emotional reactions that are stimulated by the thoughts and perceptions of our head when it is operating by itself (without a heart connection) are very limited in their vision and wisdom. We end up not perceiving the whole picture because we do not engage a major part of our intelligence, that part which sees and understands the whole. We access this additional domain of our intelligence through our hearts. The heart has the ability to see with the "eyes of Spirit" and the wisdom to understand the deeper consequences and options that lie before us. In order to engage the heart, we must put ourselves in a frequency related to love. In other words, we must attune to God.

This ability to understand from a broader perspective, to see our situations with wisdom and expanded intelligence is known by many names in the different spiritual traditions. My favorite description of this ability we all possess is Dr. Emilie Cady's term "spiritual understanding." In her book *Lessons in Truth*,[4] this turn-of-the-century healer and teacher identifies how we connect with this ability. She says:

> Understanding is a spiritual birth, a revelation of God within the heart of man.

It is not through a particular belief system or religion that the attunement takes place in which we choose the Divine to "be our God." People from many different belief systems and many people without a formal belief structure experience the gift of this wisdom, understanding, and direction through attunement to God by the activity of their love. For it is by love itself that this attunement takes place. Love stimulates the electromagnetic field of the heart, the receiver and conveyor of this intelligence. It activates the higher blueprints of our own soul patterns that give expression to the care and fulfillment inherent to the Master Law of Attunement.

When Jane surrendered her perceptions of her husband and focused on feeling love in her heart, which she was able to do by remembering the experience with her children, she attuned to that greater wisdom, her spiritual understanding or greater intelligence. Through the Law of Love and the Law of Divine Relationship she became receptive to divine wisdom showing her how to successfully deal with the upsetting situation in her relationship.

UNIVERSAL GUIDANCE

I was recently involved in training a group of corporate leaders. They were learning a way of bringing greater wisdom into their decision-making abilities. They were not of any particular religion, and several of them professed no religious belief. Yet each person was able to feel the care, appreciation, or compassion that activated the heart field, and each received clear meaningful guidance in response to his or her questions. They readily acknowledged that guidance as superior to the insights they had experienced at other times. They were very excited by this wisdom.

One of these was a Christian from a Pentecostal church. He later expressed to me that this was very similar to the guidance he had experienced when he would sincerely pray and praise

God and ask for God's direction. Because of his faith and the support of his religious training, he understood this experience in terms of God's response to him. He knew that he could bring this wisdom into many areas of his life and expand his faith because of it.

BEE—JOURNEY TO RUSSIA

In the midst of a very busy life, a woman named Bee began to recognize that she had a deep desire to go to the Soviet Union. She did not have the money for such a trip, but pursuing a personal relationship with the people of this country, who were at that time viewed as the hostile enemy, felt important to her. Because her life was so full, she found it hard to conceptualize that this was hers to do. She spoke to a friend and wondered if she should ask for a sign. Her friend responded that it was Bee who had taught her to make a commitment first and then the signs would come. Bee recognized that she did have it backward and the sign she was seeking was the desire within her own heart. This had already been given. She knew that if this were her true heart's desire, all she would need would be provided.

She said yes to the trip and immediately thereafter several friends came forward to tell her they had wonderful ideas to help her finance the trip. Another friend said, "I was waiting for you to say you wanted to go. I will pay your deposit and mine because I want to go with you." The signs came as the generous response of the universe to Bee's desire, and she became one of those early pioneers to travel and find friendship beyond the Iron Curtain. For a number of years after that, Bee assisted many other people who had that same dream in their hearts as they made similar journeys.

Bee had looked for many years at different ways to establish a deep relationship with the Divine. So when she experienced this desire in her heart, she was once again in the process of accepting that intuitive guidance instructing her in the next step for her life. She had built that internal relationship—the Divine Relationship. Her God was guiding her, and as she accepted that guidance, the money and time she needed were easily provided. Bee was experiencing the Master Law of Attunement at the personal level, the Law of Divine Relationship. She was making the decision to allow infinite wisdom and power to guide her life and provide for her needs. If you will be mine, I will be your God.

The difference between using the heart intelligence to guide the intellect and using the head's intelligence disassociated from the heart is the difference between doing something under divine guidance and doing something by one's self. When Bee was waiting for a sign, she was trying to figure things out from her head, looking for something to analyze. When she listened to her heart, she attuned herself to God's direction and care. Cayce referred to listening to your head as "your own power" as opposed to responding to God's direction and care. The broader, deeper perception and discernment of the heart allows us to bring the wisdom of God into expression in our lives. We are not bad or wrong if we do not utilize that wisdom; however, we are much less effective and are far more likely to create serious problems for ourselves through poor decisions and actions because of our limited vision. The biblical reference to this condition is in the beautiful dissertation on love where the apostle Paul says, "If I . . . can fathom all mysteries and all knowledge . . . but have not love, I am nothing." (I Corinthians 13:2 NIV)

Another understanding of Cayce's description of this law is that you do not have to be subject to the vicissitudes, the trials, troubles, turmoils of the world in which you live. You can live **in** the world but **not be of** the world. Just switch your channel. Attune yourself to the higher consciousness of Spirit. The Cayce readings sometimes refer to us as children of God, as in this excerpt which speaks powerfully of the personal reality that you can experience through tuning to a higher channel than that of the world in which you live:

> And yet it is the heritage of every soul to awake to that consciousness that God indeed is mindful of the children of men, and calls ever, "If you will be my children, I will be your God."
> This is the message, then, that you shall carry; for there is a loving Father that cares. That is your message!
> There *is;* for you have experienced it, you can and you may experience it in your *own* life!
> Can anything, any experience, any condition be more worthwhile? That, though there are those things that make men afraid, there are turmoils in this or that direction in the relationships of human experience that may terrify you for the moment, there is *He* who cares! And He may walk and talk with you!

That you may experience in your own life! *Do* that. (254-95)AR

That is what attunement is all about. You can achieve it if you choose. You can experience it personally.

BEING TAKEN CARE OF

The Master Law of Attunement implies quite clearly that if we choose to depend on ourselves—our wills, our ideas, manipulating the outer or controlling it, or putting our faith in what is going on around us—that is all we have; but, *if we put our faith and trust in the Creative Forces, we will be taken care of.*

Does that mean we will never have difficulties if we make Him our God? Often this is our concept of being taken care of. I do not believe this is true, and I have not seen this to be true in the lives of other people I have known. I understand this teaching to mean that we will have access to that infinite wisdom and love in meeting the problems and challenges that appear in our lives. In Cayce's words, "He will walk and talk with us."

Those who have consciously used this law met the problems and challenges of their lives not only with wisdom but with an ever-growing amount of love and support from those around them. Even in very difficult tribulation, they seemed to feel a state of grace. This is of course the lawful result of a life spent seeking to give expression to the love that is in their hearts. Looking at even the simplest form of Universal Law, the Law of Attraction—like attracts like—it is easy to see why this love and support would manifest.

I have known many people who have sought to live in attunement through this law. They have not lived without challenge; however, the drama and frequency of their challenges have lessened as they listened to the divine wisdom guiding their lives and as they gave expression to the deeper and deeper love they found within their hearts. The amount of joyful and meaningful time has also increased consistently as they have used this law.

FUZZY MATH

If we sincerely seek to live more and more from the heart, why do we still continue to experience challenges in our life and occasionally painful experiences? Knowing that the laws are accurate and operate everywhere with the same precision of mathematics, we, your authors, have observed many individuals' life experiences in identifying and classifying these laws. We observed the laws working accurately again and again, yet sometimes a painful or difficult situation would occur that did not seem to be the natural result of the causes we were able to witness. Both of us have had conscious recollections of situations where we created difficulties for ourselves in prior experiences in the earth, so we were aware that these could be the cause for such occurrences. However, we intuitively questioned whether such prior life situations could explain all of the cases that we observed.

We had the opportunity to talk with Doc Lew Childre, who had grown in his own love connection to the point where divine intelligence and understanding were open before him. We explained our question, and he confirmed the mathematical accuracy of the law. Then he explained the phenomenon we were observing as "fuzzy math." Fuzzy math is where the blueprint of the soul overrides the forces of the law that have been in motion. It is not a violation of the law, rather it is the expression of a higher dimensional aspect of the law.

In *Your Life: Why It Is the Way It Is and What You Can Do About It* Bruce addressed this aspect of the law as the Law of Choice— "life is the experience of our choices." Some of the choices that affect our lives are choices of the soul to develop our nature through that which is the most expedient and efficient. Sometimes this occurs when our soul finds the greater power and meaning that is within our being by going through experiences that appear to be adverse. In this case the math of the law, which is very precise in its results, appears to us to be fuzzy. However, the power of love activating a higher blueprint of the soul is choosing a more meaningful experience for that being.

IN ADVERSITY

I observed the reality of this great law, "If you will be my people, I will be your God," in the midst of an experience that appeared to be fuzzy math and that many could call tragic. It was our families' experience, yet this book which you are now reading and the understandings of the laws it teaches were at the core of the experience. Because you are a part of that family, I share this experience with you.

My father and I had begun work on this book. We had collaborated on his first book and explored and studied for many years the Universal Laws, their levels, interrelationships, and how they manifest. He and I had decided to write this book together and had each written substantial portions of it. Bruce received guidance to set the writing aside for a month and simply do those things that gave his heart pleasure. He had worked extensively on the Universal Laws for many years, writing, researching, and lecturing. This month apart was something he seldom allowed himself.

During that month he spent time with his wife, children, and grandchildren, took walks in the beautiful North Carolina mountains that were his home, and went to visit the Institute of HeartMath and its founder, Doc Lew Childre. Doc's wisdom and friendship had special meaning for Bruce. Bruce recognized the importance of the understandings and applications of the heart connection to the Universal Laws that Doc's work was bringing to people. Toward the end of that month he learned that a physical condition he had worked with for some time had expanded to a more acute level. The physical problem was cancer and working with it through diet, daily spiritual disciplines, and medical assistance had been a part of his life for several years. The cancer had served as a stimulus for him to review his own understanding of health, of the laws, and of how they related to the body and his own spiritual disciplines. Although it had slowed him down a little, it was not painful and his life had been normal in many ways.

With the sudden acceleration of the cancer's growth, the family came together to support him in that experience. We knew that total healing was an option that could manifest just as death and transition from his body could also manifest. A major part of the inner work Bruce undertook at that point was to go deep within his heart to receive clearly the guidance and wisdom that were there and to surrender to that love. He was willing to respond to whatever that inner direction was. For a while, that seemed to be to heal the body, so those things he could do to support his body in its healing he did, from prayer to medical assistance. And then the inner direction changed. He understood that this was about the death of the body and his transition from the earth plane. At that point, filled with a great sense of love, he peacefully surrendered to that process. His conscious focus became simply feeling the love and care that filled each moment. His family gathered around and when all had gathered, he gently made his transition.

I share this story with you because this was a person who knew the Law of Divine Relationship intimately. He had a spent large portion of his life seeking to understand what it meant to be a child of God and acknowledging and developing his relationship to God. Yet he was not spared sickness and death, for that is not the care that Bruce was speaking of earlier when he wrote, *"if we put our trust in the Creative Forces, we will be taken care of."* Rather, as I saw in his life, this care meant that there was the wisdom, the strength, and the guidance to meet each situation in a way that resulted in growth, meaning, and fulfillment. A gentle grace prevailed throughout this experience of illness. Indeed, so great was the love around all of us at his death that it was often difficult to feel the grief of parting. The sense of accomplishment and celebration for his completion of a life of value and contribution and the power of our love for him were so great that there were more smiles than tears and more appreciation than regret. It was a holy time of great meaning and love. Truly he and all of us were cared for.

A PURE AND SIMPLE RELATIONSHIP

It is simple. As you put the One God first, then He will care for you as one of His people—if not, you are on your own. Moses gave the Master Law of Attunement to his people thousands of years ago. The Old Testament is the history of how those people found joy, peace, and happiness when they lived as His people and how they were enslaved and suffered when they ignored this Universal Law. This law has not changed over time. It still applies to you and me here and now—this day: If you will be my people, I will be your God.

The Master Law of Attunement leaves it strictly up to us; there is no implication of demand or requirement. We are left to exercise our free will as we choose. And if we do choose to accept this relationship, then Spirit is bound to that relationship by this law and becomes our source and our supply for as long as we choose to maintain and live in accord with that consciousness.

Are there some "hooks" in this? What is required of us? There is only the requirement that we attune ourselves to Spirit instead of to the power of the world. Along with that requirement goes an incredible guarantee that is a far better deal than you can get anywhere else. It is a guarantee because it is a law. It is the second Law of Attunement.[5]

THE LAW OF SEEKING FIRST

Do we wish for our beloved . . . is there aught else for which we long, yet for all our longing do not obtain? Lo, all shall be ours if we but dive deep within, even to the lotus of the heart, where dwells the Lord.

Chandogya Upanishad[6]

The Law of Seeking First—"Seek first the Spirit within and all you have need of will be added."

If you need a house, a car, a mate, a dog, a new job, understanding, emotional balance, or more money, seek first the Spirit within and all you have need of will be added. This is very practical advice. Does that mean someone will drive up and give you the keys to a new car? It has happened, but, like winning the lottery, it is not the way this law usually works. What the law provides is guidance and facilitation so that we live in ever-increasing effectiveness in the physical, mental, emotional, social, and spiritual aspects of our lives.

SEEKING SPIRIT FIRST

Note the requirement that we seek first, which is to say we make this search the first priority in our lives. One of the great challenges of the spiritual laws is that they can sound as though they are machines, that one can turn a crank and have a particular result instantly drop out of the spout into one's life. This is not the way they work. The laws themselves are living dynamics of life that are attuned to each individual's life. They integrate the entire range of that individual's life, conscious and subconscious. This makes a tremendous difference when we speak of seeking "first," because outer rules of what first means are far less valid than understanding the "attitude of first."

For instance, it's easy to think of God first in the morning or immediately offer up a prayer or thought of God when you have a question or challenge. This can be very helpful, yet misleading in the understanding of how the law really works. First is less about "when," than it is about "how." First for one person may be when he or she is deeply immersed in a problem and remembers that there is a higher knowledge and power, then with joy turns the focus to that love. For another person, it may begin long before a challenge or need arises, with appreciation of the beauty of the green of the leaves on the trees as the person drives to work.

First is the description of the sincerity of a relationship, rather than time, place, or technique. First describes the depth of heart feeling about that Spirit within rather than a form or routine. I had a friend who told me her experience with a priest who was about to leave a gathering at her house and go home to meditate. She asked him if he weren't disappointed at having to leave this gathering of friends to spend time in his discipline. His response was that going home to this inner time, this inner connection, was like "going home to his beloved." In his life that Spirit within was first.

People who have become very diligent in their personal practices have asked me, "Why doesn't this law work for me?" When I looked at their lives, what I saw missing was the depth of heart. They did turn to that Spirit in their minds but without the touch of wisdom and attunement that comes through the heart. I have also seen people who were unaware of this law but whose love and sincerity brought all that they needed constantly into their lives in simple and profound ways.

I have the very special opportunity of working with a group of people to whom this inner Spirit is first in their lives. They are from many religious backgrounds, from Southern Baptists to yoga teachers, and some with no real religious affiliation. Yet I can say that for each one the relationship with that inner Spirit is first for them because of their commitment to loving. They seek diligently to meet the situations in their lives with the power of the heart—not the syrupy sentimental heart of greeting cards and television but the heart of wisdom, intelligence, and sincere care. What I have seen manifest in their lives is not great wealth. Their lives are financially quite modest. However, every need is taken care of in some simple way, and the inner quality of their life experience is far, far beyond what millions of dollars could even hope to buy.

Many ways exist to keep that relationship with Spirit first in our lives: regular practices of prayer and meditation; the support of life in a community of worship such as a church, study group, ashram, or synagogue; techniques that focus our attention on God such as affirmation, scripture reading, daily devotions, and tithing. Certainly tithing is one of the most effective because it acknowledges that relationship at the physical, mental, and spiritual levels. All of these are helpful, yet in doing these things, it is the depth of connection in your heart that brings the true potential of this law into expression.

TWO MUSLIM MEN

I met two devout Muslim men in Jerusalem on the same day. Although they both lived in similar circumstances, one expressed his hatred of those who were not Muslim and criticized every one around him, from the Jews he lived near to the others of his own faith and family who believed differently than he did.

The other man seemed joyous and contented. He spoke with great understanding of others who shared his faith but held different views. He told me of being arrested by Israeli soldiers and singing songs to them in praise of Moses as he was taken to prison. He spoke of those who had imprisoned him with love, care, and understanding. The quality of his life was totally different from the life of the first man, yet both were people of sincere devotion to the disciplines of their faith. The difference that I experienced between them was the difference of putting Spirit first. Instead of that "first" being an outer discipline, the "first" for the second man meant focusing first on the heart and the feeling of love. His life had grown in love and he was surrounded by all the things that fulfilled his heart—friends, family, and community. Even when he was arrested, he was able to move through those challenges with wisdom and grace. His seeking was from his heart—with and through love.

NEEDS

The law speaks of needs rather than wants. Needs are not limited to survival; in fact, needs can include great wealth. If it is a part of your desire to care for others, your family, or to accomplish a certain mission, you may need wealth. To others it is not a need. Health is a need for many, yet some have chosen to learn through an illness. What is needed in that situation may be the learning that is even more valuable than the physical health.

With the Puritan background of our country and the many religious movements that have focused on world denial rather than world appreciation, many people associate a spiritual life with poverty. However, everything is an expression of frequencies. Wealth and the material world are simply a range of frequencies that we can experience and enjoy. Yet many who have sought to work with this law have had to go through experiences of poverty. At those times when the individual released his or her dependence on material things, such as the bank account or the plan of how things would be provided, all that was really needed appeared. The unanticipated provision demonstrated far more effectively than money in the bank the power of this law: Seek first the Spirit within, and you will be provided with all you have need of. Remember to listen to that inner guidance, the still, small voice, the heart intuitive response. It may be the greatest provision.

This law operates to bring the love of Spirit into manifested form because it utilizes the pattern of creation expressed in the Law of Manifestation—"Spirit is the life, mind is the builder, the physical is the result." It works to bring us not only our mental and physical needs but also the experience of fulfillment which is available to us when we attune ourselves to the Spirit within us. To fully utilize this law, it is important that we learn to listen to the wisdom of Spirit directing our lives so that we can receive the fulfillment of our needs. This wisdom is within our hearts and easily accessible, as described in the chapters on the "Law of Wisdom" and "How to Love."

As we attune to that divine presence and receive its provision through spiritual energy and intelligence, our world changes because we have energized a higher pattern of our reality. Reality is not the fixed thing we believe it to be; rather it is a process of selecting different frequency patterns through our thoughts, feelings, beliefs, and actions. When those patterns are energized, they express themselves in our inner and outer worlds. We have often tried to do this through mental energy or emotional energy as we struggled to manifest an ideal or goal we held. Seeking first is using the heart to bring the spiritual energy into our lives that can easily energize a pattern attuned to our purpose and help manifest that pattern in our lives.

As you work with this wonderful law, allow it to bring to you the true needs of your soul. Seek first the Spirit within and allow it to bring to you and guide you to receive the desires of your heart at all levels—mental, emotional, social, spiritual, and physical.

Chapter 5

How to Love

The Lord God, all-pervading and omnipresent, dwells in the heart of all beings. Full of grace, he ultimately gives liberation to all creatures by turning their faces toward himself.
                                                            Svetasvatara

God is love.   1 John 4:16

How to love. It seems like such a simple idea. You know how to love, don't you? Every one of us has loved. You have cared deeply about someone with strong feelings, so yes, you do know how to love.

I too have loved. However, as I sought to apply the Law of Love in my life, I discovered that I didn't know how to choose love at will. It wasn't there when I needed it. It was something that just happened sometimes. It certainly wasn't available to me when I was in a state of anger, pain, or fear. As I worked with many other people, assisting them in using the Law of Love to transform their painful situations, I found that very few people were able to choose to love. It is hard to love someone who has been negative toward us, especially if that person has caused deep hurt or pain.

A CARING TEACHER

When I think of how to apply the Law of Love, I think of

Melinda, a teacher who found herself in a very difficult professional position. She had decided to work with a child we will call Matt, a young boy whom she had accepted into her classroom on a trial basis. On the first day of school Matt lost control the first time she confronted him with his inappropriate behavior toward another child. He began to scream and kick and lash out physically and verbally at anyone and anything in his path. Melinda had to physically remove him from the classroom. Once outside Matt turned all his rage on her. She ended up with two deep bites on her arms, a black eye, and bruises on both her legs.

This became the pattern of a lot of days with Matt. At the same time she and the director of education were working with the parents. One of their recommendations included evaluation and counseling with a therapist.

After weeks of this, Melinda was drained, frustrated, and ready to give up. All she wanted, at this point, was the calm and peaceful class she had when Matt was not there. For some inexplicable reason she postponed a meeting with the director of education that she knew was going to result in the school asking Matt to leave. Instead Melinda went home and worked with some techniques she had learned that enabled her to connect with the intuitive intelligence and wisdom of her heart. She knew to look to love for the answer, not only from her training in the heart techniques through HeartMath and her spiritual background but also because she had studied this wisdom from Dr. Maria Montessori's writings. In a section of *The Secret of Childhood* titled "Intelligence of Love," she had read:

> The whole labor of life which fulfills itself subject to its law and brings beings into harmony reaches consciousness under the form of love. It is love which unites the child to things. It is not love in the sense that is commonly understood as an emotional feeling, but a love of the intelligence which sees and assimilates and builds itself through loving. Yes, the inner guide that leads children to observe what is about them could be described, in Dante's phrase, as "intelligence of love." Is it not a characteristic of love, that sensibility that enables a child to see what others do not see? That collects details the others do not perceive, and appreciates special qualities, which are, as it were, hidden, and which love can discover? It is because the child's intel-

ligence assimilates by loving, and not just indifferently, that he can see the invisible. This active, ardent, meticulous, constant absorption in love is characteristic of children.[1]

To apply her love to the situation before her, she connected with her heart through the technique of Freeze-Frame. It was a powerful experience, and she was surprised at the action plan that resulted. Melinda knew clearly that her heart was telling her to try to reach Matt's heart.

On Monday morning she took Matt out for a ride in his wheel-chair. (He had fallen from a tree.) They sat under some pine trees, and she told him about his heart. He asked a lot of questions and seemed very interested and thoughtful about what she was telling him. She taught him how to use the tool of Freeze-Frame so that he could get to his heart when he felt out of control.

From that day on, Matt tried very hard to use Freeze-Frame and she began to see dramatic results. His screaming and physical abuse began to abate. His parents reported the same results at home. Matt told his friends about Freeze-Frame and even taught his parents.

Matt did eventually leave the school, but Melinda had the satisfaction of having given Matt a new way to work with his life. From her love, she had found what it was he needed and had given him the gift of being able to connect with his own love. Matt's world changed because Melinda loved him enough to teach him how to connect with his own heart. Melinda's world changed as well. Because she had turned to specific ways to utilize her love and care in dealing with this very difficult child, she brought greater fulfillment to her experience as a teacher, and she discovered how effective the transforming intelligence of her heart was in turning a hopeless experience of growing loss and failure into success for all concerned.

This experience is particularly meaningful to me in looking at how to love because it shatters so many of the perceptions we have about love. Love is not the syrupy material of Valentine cards. It is a powerful, intelligent force that unleashes through the Law of Love the very creative energy of the universe. It doesn't require twenty years of meditation or a particular religious background. Even an emotionally difficult six year old can use it. It changes those who use it and those to whom it is directed. Love transforms.

LEARNING TO LOVE

In order to utilize the Law of Love for personal transformation, it is necessary to love ourselves and others. However, there are parts of ourselves we do not like, just like there are types of people we do not like. Sometimes an inner aspect of ourselves has caused us a lot of trouble. How can we love it? We may have succeeded in life by controlling that part of ourselves, but not by loving it.

Remember Victoria's experience with little Vicki? If someone had just ruined our entry into a career for which we had been preparing ourselves for years, we would probably be very angry. Anger is a natural protective response. Yet, in order to transform her situation, Victoria had to bring her love to this aspect of herself—little Vicki—that had acted in a childish manner before the committee.

When we discover how little we know about consciously directing our love and how difficult it is to call upon our love in painful circumstances, it is easy to understand why people have not utilized more extensively the transforming power of the Law of Love. In addition, our word *love* is a very confusing term. We apply it to many of the very powerful emotions that we associate with romantic love, although some of those emotions are not love at all. They can be security needs, sexual desire, self-worth feelings, sentimentality, and often obsessive needs to possess or control another person. Thus people are legitimately skeptical of love as an answer to their problems. These associations and the lack of knowledge of how to use our love are more than enough reason for most people to dismiss talk of loving as sentimental nonsense.

Feelings of love are stimulated by the movement of spiritual energy through the heart. There are many feelings that are felt in the heart but do not originate there. Even anger or hatred, which is not from the heart but created from specific head perceptions connected to strong emotional energy, can be felt to some degree in the heart because there may be elements of self-care and value behind the emotional passion. Core heart feelings such as appreciation, care, compassion, forgiveness, courage, kindness, and peace originate from the movement of Spirit through the heart as does love. Each of those are an expression of an aspect of love. People have sometimes assumed all emotions and feelings come from the heart. However, only those transformative feelings activate the higher functions of the heart. Negative feelings actually shut down the sensitivity of the heart. The release from the negative feelings comes about through the reactivation of the heart.

Love is not sentimental, although it is sensitive, and it is not the associated feelings of security that may be triggered in a personal relationship, although it does bring a sense of security to the individual. Love is a spiritual experience, whether it is in the midst of romance, motherly love, a sense of brotherhood, caring about others, love of God, or a commitment to an ideal. It is possible to love when we want to, to love the repugnant parts of ourselves, and to love others at moments we don't even like them. It is possible to learn to love. In so doing we are opening ourselves to enter a spiritual experience at will.

THE HEART

The association we have all heard between love and the heart is an accurate one. Do you remember looking into the eyes of that special someone and sincerely saying, "I love you with all my head!"? Of course not. It is through our spiritual center we call the heart that we feel the movement of the divine presence as love. There are other spiritual centers in the body; however, the heart is the balance point for the energy that flows through all of them. The heart is the center of the intelligence that effectively manages the distribution of energy through all the centers. When our energy is centered in the heart, we are able to consciously work with the energy of our love.

There are several situations in which it is helpful to know how to direct your love:

The FIRST is in transforming daily thoughts and feelings.

The SECOND is to heal or transform painful emotional memories to eliminate limiting emotional patterns and beliefs from your life.

The THIRD is how to send your love in support of the transformation of others.

TRANSFORM THOUGHTS AND FEELINGS

How can you direct your love to transform daily thoughts and feelings? From the Laws of Cause and Effect, we know that our thoughts and feelings are of tremendous importance in determining what is going to take place in our lives. Positive thoughts do assist in maintaining positive feelings; however, many of the habitual patterns of our thoughts and feelings are deeply ingrained, and it becomes difficult to maintain a positive attitude in spite of our best intentions. Knowing how to transform (rather than simply switch) negative thoughts and feelings in our daily lives gives us the ability not only to make a different choice but also to transform, or release, the lower pattern and establish the higher pattern as our norm.

By examining the electromagnetic properties of the heart, we can discover the frequency signature of love and the relationship of specific feeling or frequency patterns in transformation.

ECG PATTERN

Science has known for some time that emotions and attitudes affect the electrical signal of the heart, as shown in the following graph:

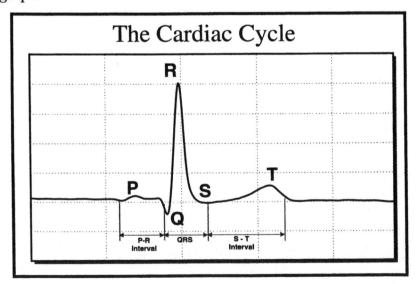

Figure 5A

Fig. 5A. This is the electrical signal generated by the heart each time it beats, as recorded in an electrocardiogram (ECG). Emotions such as anger, anxiety, and depression make changes that are observable in this electrical signal, which is a composite of the electrical energies in the heart. Feelings such as anger cause depression of the T wave, and feelings of depression cause a widening of the Q, R, S complex.

The above wave form is the result of many individual frequencies that combine to make this familiar pattern. If we break this signal down into its component frequencies, we get graphs, like figs. 5B and 5C below, which show each one of the frequencies that is being generated by our hearts. Looking at this graph is like looking at a radio. Each one of the vertical lines along the horizontal axis is a different frequency being generated from the heart, just like each line of a radio dial is a distinct radio frequency.

ECG SPECTRUM—FRUSTRATION

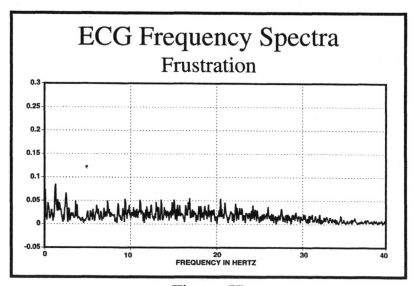

Figure 5B

Figs. 5B and 5C show the spectrum analysis of eight seconds of ECG data while feeling frustrated (5B) and while feeling sincere appreciation (5C). The chaotic pattern produced by frustration in 5B is called an incoherent spectrum. The ordered pattern produced by sincere appreciation in 5C is called a coherent spectrum.[2]

When you are feeling the emotion of frustration, your heart generates a similar pattern of frequencies. That pattern also looks like the seismographic recording of a California earthquake—and feels like it on the inside. This chaotic pattern is called an incoherent frequency spectra. In it, many of the wave patterns are interfering with each other and canceling each other out. The result is similar to turning on your radio and getting static on every station.

ECG SPECTRUM—APPRECIATION

If you were to enter into a deep feeling of appreciation, you would be experiencing a part of the feeling of love. Love is expressed through many feelings such as appreciation, care, or compassion. When you sincerely feel appreciation, the power of love is transforming the electrical pattern being generated by the heart. The new pattern looks like this:

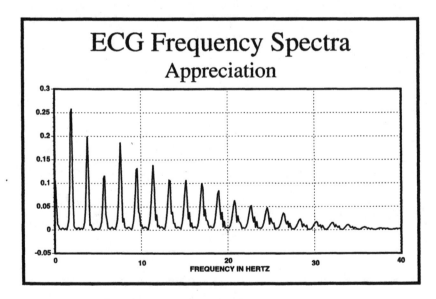

Figure 5C

Fig. 5C shows the coherent frequency pattern generated by the heart while feeling sincere appreciation. The ordered pattern is a harmonic series. Notice the greater power (the vertical axes) in fig. 5C as compared to fig. 5B.[3]

Here we see order, harmony, and power expressed in the frequency pattern. This is like playing a beautiful chord on the piano, where the above graph of frustration was like striking the piano with your whole arm. We can see by the change in the electrical system of the heart a much higher, more efficient level of operation than when frustration was expressed. Love transforms.

There are a number of feelings or attitudes that generate a coherent frequency pattern in the signature of love. If, for example, you were to feel sincere care while hooked up to an electrocardiograph and that information were run through a computer that converted the data to a frequency spectrum, the computer would print out a coherent wave pattern like the one in fig. 5C. A coherent wave pattern appears as evenly spaced wave peaks on the paper. The coherent wave pattern is the electromagnetic signature of love.

If you were at work and something you thought you needed right away wasn't happening—maybe a phone call—and you were reacting with a feeling of frustration, then your computer printout would be a lot of incoherent peaks like fig. 5B.

We can consciously choose to change from the incoherent pattern to the healthy, ordered, coherent pattern by moving our energy into the heart and entering into one of the feelings that are a part of the love frequency.

TRANSFORMING FRUSTRATION

Let's return to the example at the office and the phone call you need that isn't coming through. You recognize your feeling of frustration and take a moment to look around the room. You spot another employee who helped you on a difficult project the other day. Then you begin to appreciate that employee, thinking of her skill and her articulateness which was of particular assistance to you in that project.

What is happening internally is that your new attitude of appreciation has begun drawing your energy into your heart. You are changing from a chaotic pattern to the beautifully ordered, coherent frequency pattern of love (fig. 5C). You are also beginning to build your energy. While you were in frustration, you were depleting yourself of energy and building up stress. With your thoughts of appreciation drawing energy through your heart, you are regenerating your energy.

You would only see the frequencies change if you sincerely felt appreciation. Merely thinking thoughts of apprecation won't make the change. This is why so many positive thought programs are of such limited effect. The Law of Love does not operate on thoughts of love. It only operates on feelings of love.

Your new attitude is transforming the internal reactive pattern that was creating the negative energy of your frustration. The positive energy of your love is drawing to you the solutions you need. Perhaps the phone will ring—you are centered and ready to respond. Perhaps another alternative will occur to you. When you are in the positive feelings and energy of the love vibration, you are operating at a higher level, so the world you are creating is at a higher level because like attracts like.

FREEZE-FRAME

In the midst of negative emotional feelings, how do you make the switch to love? Most of us would find it very difficult to start feeling love. What we can do is select a specific frequency that generates the coherent wave pattern of love. In the above example, I used the feeling of appreciation stimulated by the thought of another person's assistance. You might find it helpful to recall a fun-filled moment when your heart came alive. That might be when the beauty of nature touched your deep sense of appreciation or your grandson held out his arms to you.

These feelings stimulate the electromagnetic field around the heart and produce the coherent wave pattern of love. Each feeling is an aspect of love that invokes the transforming power of the Law of Love. It is the feeling that brings about the change— the shift in the heart—not merely the thought. I used to try to make this shift by selecting only positive thoughts and discovered how difficult it was to manage the head with the head. I wanted to feel love, but often I thought I was feeling love when in fact I was only thinking love. This attempt was particularly helpful in that it moved me from a stressed, reactive framework into a more neutral one. However, it was a long way from the transformation possible through the Law of Love.

Then I learned the process of Freeze-Frame taught by Doc Lew Childre in his book *Freeze-Frame: Fast Action Stress Relief.* To be honest, I almost did not learn it because it appeared too simple and I thought, "I already know all that." Fortunately I tried the process using the steps as he gave them and discovered that his unique combination of steps brought this transformational process into an easy, user-friendly sequence that was far more effective than what I and others had been doing. Instead of using my earlier more cumbersome method, I requested his permission to share his steps with you directly:

The Steps of Freeze-Frame

1. Recognize the stressful feeling, and Freeze-Frame it. Take a time-out!

2. Make a sincere effort to shift your focus away from the racing mind or disturbed emotions to the area around your heart. Pretend you're breathing through your heart to help focus your energy in this area. Keep your focus there for ten seconds or more.

3. Recall a positive, fun feeling or time you've had in life and attempt to reexperience it.

4. Now, using your intuition, common sense, and sincerity— ask your heart, what would be a more efficient response to the situation, one that will minimize future stress?

5. Listen to what your heart says in answer to your question. (It's an effective way to put your reactive mind and emotions in check – and an "in-house" source of common-sense solutions!)[4]

You may want to practice doing Freeze-Frame with your eyes closed the first few times while you get the feeling for it. It only takes a minute or two. Part of the beauty of the Freeze-Frame technique is that you can use it with your eyes open, face-to-face with the difficulties that occur in life.

A MEDICAL SITUATION

We had moved to the Santa Cruz area only a few months before my wife developed a medical problem. It resulted in her having to go into a local outpatient surgery for a minor operation. It was a financial stretch for us because we were not yet covered by insurance, but we knew the operation was important and those things would work out. I was in the waiting room when the doctor came out with his surgical mask and other apparel on and called me into the hallway. There he began explaining to me that he had stopped the operation because the condition was much more severe than he had anticipated. It required a far more extensive operation because a risk to my wife's life was involved.

As he was talking, my mind began to comprehend the magnitude of the difficulty confronting us. I had been through the death of a spouse and his words triggered fears of that loss plus the worry about the overwhelming financial disaster for which we were not at all prepared. I suddenly became aware of the stressful situation I was in and the thoughts and feelings that were active in my mind. I wanted to be clear at this very important moment, so I chose to Freeze-Frame.

First, being aware of my thoughts and feelings, I took a time out on the thinking I was doing, like pressing the pause button on a VCR.

Secondly, I focused my attention on the area around my heart and pretended I was breathing through that area for 10 seconds or more.

Thirdly, I needed a strong, positive heart feeling. Because of the nature of the situation I was in, I couldn't think of one that was fun; however, I could genuinely feel deep appreciation for this doctor who was standing in front of me. He had used his skill to recognize a problem, made the decision that was most responsive to my wife's health, and come out immediately to inform me fully of what was going on. In a moment I was aware of these things as I focused my attention on my appreciation of him until I felt it sincerely in my heart area.

Next came the important fourth step in which I silently asked my heart, "What is the most efficient response to this situation — one that will minimize future stress?"

As I listened to my heart, the response was an immediate awareness that none of the things about death and money that I had been thinking about were important in this moment. The only thing that was of real importance to me was that my wife would be aware of all of this because she had only had a local anesthetic. She would be very frightened and needed my love and support. It was so clear to me that this was what was important that my thoughts did not return to the other issues. I felt a sense of clarity, care, and strength. I had been aware of everything the doctor had said during the thirty seconds I had been doing the Freeze-Frame, and now I was ready to complete that conversation and go to my wife.

Fortunately, a week later when the full surgery took place, some of the complications that the doctor had realized were a possibility were not present. My wife is now healthy and living a full, active life. We were able to handle the financial challenges and are successfully through that difficulty, very grateful for the good care we received at many levels.

I share this experience with you because Freeze-Frame is a tool that you can use right in the middle of situations such as this one that are very stressful and difficult. Many people have told me of using it successfully in meetings or confrontations where emotions were high and very important projects and relationships were at stake. Others have acknowledged that they wished they would have remembered to Freeze-Frame but did remember afterward and still found it helpful in letting go of their stress from the meeting and seeing clearly the best course to follow.

As you use the steps of Freeze-Frame, you will find that it gets quicker and easier. It can be used eyes open in the moment of stress when our reactive mind starts to do its thing. It can also be beneficial during a quiet moment while programs are changing on the computer, or just before going into a meeting or before getting out of the car.

Freeze-Frame is a tool that is successful because it utilizes the Law of Love. "Love transforms." The power of the heart is a help in the stressful situations of life, but this tool's use goes far beyond these situations. Use Freeze-Frame in the moments when things are good, when you are enjoying a project at work, or when you are together with people you love. Love transforms good moments, giving them a greater texture and quality that expands enjoyment of the blessings that divine love brings into your life. Go for all the goodness you can get. Our hearts are designed not only to lead us out of our pain and difficulty but also to bring an ever-expanding goodness into our experience. It is the doorway to heaven on earth.

HEART AND INTELLECT

Some people have legitimate questions about going to their hearts. What if we have jobs that demand an intellectual response? Isn't the heart too sentimental for the workplace? What if intellectual acuity is needed?

The heart is not filled with sentiment. The heart energy actually enhances the intellectual capacity of an individual. It assists us in moving beyond limiting emotional patterns to view a situation accurately.

There is the well-known nerve pathway from the head to the heart through the autonomic nervous system. But there is also a nerve pathway from the heart to the brain. The result of the activation of the heart energy is the stimulation of the neurocortex of the brain which is the source of our higher reasoning capacities. The brain works better when the heart is engaged.

Remember being in school and studying for a subject that you loved? Loving the subject brought your heart energies to your learning. The learning required much less effort and your understanding was heightened. Remember what it was like preparing for a class that you did not like? It was just head work, and it took a lot more work to accomplish the same degree of understanding. Love vitalizes the mind.

HEART-BRAIN ENTRAINMENT

The highly efficient state of entrainment that is brought about by the feelings of love, also effects the brain. The following graphs show frequency entrainment between the heart and brain.

The heart intelligence stimulates the brain to a higher level of effective functioning. Both the neurological pathway and the electromagnetic one shown here are important elements in accessing the higher intelligence that results when we connect with Spirit through the heart. The deeper the heart feelings we have, the higher the level of intelligence we are able to access.

Fig. 5D, right side, shows the EEG (brain wave, top) and ECG (heart signal, bottom) of an individual. The left side is before Freeze-Frame and there is no relationship between the heart and brain. On the right side after the person has activated the love feeling (coherent frequency pattern) through Freeze-Frame ("FF" on the charts). The brain wave (a signal averaged wave form) has entrained with the heart frequency. [5]

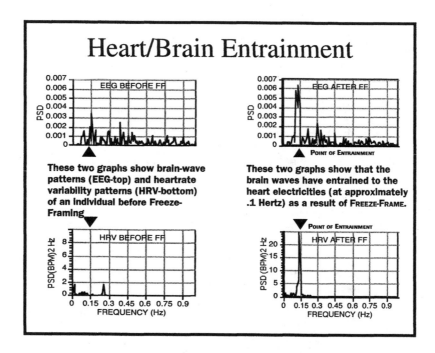

Figure 5D

NEUTRAL—A GIFT FROM THE HEART

You have just moved to a new town, a new job. It seems pretty good, but you can't find the house you want and the apartment your family is living in is really inadequate. You have come home after another Sunday of open houses with nothing that you liked in your price range and never wanting to see another house. "Maybe this wasn't the right move and we shouldn't have come." Well, it makes sense, doesn't it? "If this was right for us, things should have worked, and we would have found a house." This is a good time to go to your heart. "Chill out," as the kids say. In your heart you don't have to answer that question immediately. As you appreciate your family and think of all the effort and cooperation they each gave to this move, enjoy your love for them. Feel your love for them. Bring your question into your heart and just hold it in neutral.

Neutral is a very special place in your heart. In neutral there is no judgment, no right or wrong, just a resting while your heart enfolds the question. What happens from neutral is that you get a wider perspective. You are able to see things differently. Over the next several minutes, hours, days, however long you want to work with neutral, your perspective clears. It's like putting on prescription glasses—you can see things clearly. "Well, things weren't great where I was; at least we opened some new possibilities here. There are challenges any place. This challenge is just finding a house; at least I do have a job and I feel good about it so far." A new perspective—a gift from the neutral space in your heart.

To get to neutral is easy:

1. Focus your attention on the area around your heart.
2. Place your concern in your heart in neutral.
3. Manage your thoughts and keep them in neutral until your heart has a chance to give you a broader perspective.

APPRECIATION

Each time we give expression to a core feeling of the heart, we activate the Law of Love in that situation. Appreciation is one of the most powerful and effective frequencies of love. Let's explore the power of appreciation. I have greatly appreciated the following story which I first heard many years ago:

A man had grown very tired of his wife. Her constant nagging and complaining had driven him to the point where he decided to divorce her. He went to see the rabbi, whom he told about his great frustration and anger for all the abuse that he had received from her. The rabbi was very understanding, and noting the man's anger, asked him if he didn't want to get even with the wife for all he had suffered. The man was eager for the chance of revenge and asked the rabbi how he could get even.

The rabbi told the man to pretend and let his wife think that he thought her beautiful and loving and that he deeply appreciated her. That way, when he later divorced her, she would know what a great loss she had suffered and would realize that she could never get another husband as wonderful as he. The rabbi instructed the man to tell her every morning and evening that she was lovely and beautiful and to thank her profusely for everything she did for him, even the smallest things. The man eagerly agreed to this fiendish plot.

A year later the rabbi met the man at the market. The rabbi asked the man if he still wanted to divorce his wife. The man looked at the rabbi with surprise and said, "Why would I want to divorce such a beautiful, wonderful, and thoughtful wife?"

The rabbi had given the man the tool of appreciation. Our heart spectrum analysis assures us that appreciation only has its full power when it is used sincerely; however, the rabbi's point is well made that this is a powerful tool, and when used, changes both the person using it and the one appreciated.

If there is a relationship that is important to you, bring sincere appreciation into active expression between you. You are activating the Law of Love—"love transforms."

I remember hearing of a native culture studied by anthropologists because it had no crime. The researchers discovered that when an individual was doing something that was disruptive to others the whole village gathered and sat in a circle. Each person in turn told the offending person who was seated in the center the things they appreciated about him, the good things he had done, or his good personal qualities. When all had finished acknowledging all of the things they could think of, everyone went back to work. There was no more thought given to the disruptive behavior. The result was a culture without crime.

When I first heard this many years ago, I began to respond differently to my children's disruptive behavior. I found that genuinely appreciating the wonderful qualities they brought into my life changed the atmosphere for us. I was then able to easily understand and deal effectively with the behavioral problem. Actually, the problem often seemed unimportant, and sometimes we totally forgot to talk about it.

TRANSFORM PAINFUL EMOTIONAL MEMORIES

This understanding is one of the most important in our process of transformation. Each person has within him- or herself emotional wounds from traumatic experiences in life. These wounds are very real barriers to experiencing the fullness of love and joy that are the expression of the spiritual beings we really are. From these painful experiences we have formed beliefs that continue to manifest as difficulties in our lives through the Law of Belief.

We can heal and transform these places of emotional hurt within us by the power of our love. Whether it is an experience of physical or emotional abuse, sexual abuse, violence, or any of the subtler yet limiting experiences of disappointment and abandonment that we feel, love has the power to heal and transform that limitation.

Sara Paddison, author of *The Hidden Power of the Heart*, describes this transformation process as leaping from one picture or movie to another. She speaks of these realities in terms of their holographic nature. A hologram is a three-dimensional picture or image. Because we are living in a three-dimensional image, she refers to the process of changing our relationship to the past, and thus the future, as a "hololeap." She says:

> If you don't go to your heart and learn from misfortune, you could magnetize similar frequencies to yourself (possibly another misfortune). When you use heart intelligence in life, you rearrange your future frequencies and often can avoid disasters.
>
> From my experience, a fifth-dimensional hololeap is possible when you view your filmstrip and then have the intelligence to release or remodel part of your character. You can actually walk into the holographic heart and reenact that part in the play. In other words, you give yourself a fresh start by going into your past and making a different choice. It's like taking out a particular computer chip, an old program, by altering the basic frequency. You come back to your everyday world, but with less baggage and a fresh perspective.[6]

One example of such a change of frequency is what Victoria went through with that part of herself that was a frightened, hurt child. She found little Vicki by the feelings of fear and the childish reaction she had to that fear. Victoria remembered hiding in the corner as a frightened little Vicki while violence took place around her in her family. She altered the basic frequency of that memory by bringing the transforming power of her love to little Vicki.

We have all held painful experiences in our memory until the love response alters that basic frequency, thus freeing us to grow. To heal that pain, we can bring our love to that part of ourselves that holds the pain. For Victoria, that part of herself was the memory of herself as a little girl whom she called little Vicki.

Love transforms, so our work is to learn how to direct our love to that part of us that remembers pain or rejection. We can do this through several steps. Because this is the work of love, it is important that we approach it in a loving manner. Setting aside enough time to do this is a part of loving ourselves. If your life has a number of issues, begin to learn this process on the small ones. As you grow in skill and understanding of your own inner dynamic, allow yourself to progress to more challenging issues.

How do we transform these patterns? The following steps take us through a process that allows the power of our love to do its transforming work. It is not the only way; however, this way of transformation has been helpful for me and many people with whom I have worked. It consists of three main steps:

1. Identify the feeling.
2. Bring love to it.
3. Give thanks.

EMOTIONAL HEALING STEPS

1. Identify the feeling.

Identify the negative feeling that is disturbing you. For Victoria it was being afraid and feeling childish. Be aware of the sensations in your body and your emotions. As you expand your awareness by observing yourself, you could say, "This is what it is like when I experience this feeling." Sometimes, memories or images may want to surface, as when Victoria was remembering little Vicki. That is not necessary, but it is fine if it happens.

2. Bring love to it.

Have compassion for yourself. Bring love to yourself just as if you were the parent and your child was feeling afraid or hurt. Enfold the emotion in the love and compassion of your heart. As you deepen your feeling of love, acknowledge any thoughts of love. Perhaps—"I love you the way you are." If you have a memory, as Victoria did, bring your love to that self, send it compassion, and hold it in the warmth of your heart.

Deepen your feelings of love. Imagine that each breath is breathing your love to the feeling of hurt or fear. Be aware of your love. Enjoy the emotion that love, care, or compassion elicits.

3. Give thanks.

As you release the hurt or fear, continue sending your love. When the release feels complete, take a moment to recognize the change in how you feel. By the Law of Love, the hurt you carried has been transformed. Take a moment to sincerely feel your thankfulness for the transforming power of the love that set you free.

For complete release, the intensity of the feeling of love needs to be as strong as the intensity of the hurt. It may require additional experiences of loving to complete the release. You'll notice, if it reappears at all, that it will be diminished in intensity. That is a good time to give it another dose of love.

REBECCA—TRANSFORMING POWERLESSNESS

This is how Rebecca utilized these steps to overcome a limiting hologram of powerlessness, especially when criticized. Although she was well-educated and articulate, she was consistently passed up for advancements in her career because she lacked self-confidence. Her sense of powerlessness also plagued her in her marriage where her resentments (against others making decisions that affected her) often erupted in angry words. When Rebecca began to examine her feelings and the thoughts and beliefs about herself that were manifesting through the Law of Attraction, she identified this feeling of powerlessness. She allowed herself to experience that feeling. Accompanying that feeling was a sense of vulnerability.

For Rebecca a memory surfaced that helped her identify the feeling further. She remembered an earlier time when she had experienced that feeling. Her memory took her back to several weeks before when her boss was being unjustly critical of her work and she felt powerless to stand up for herself. Another earlier memory then surfaced of being abused by a drunk uncle. She remembered the room, her fear, embarrassment, and shame.

As she allowed herself to acknowledge those feelings, she became a friend or parent to the young girl in her memory. She blotted out the uncle and focused her attention on the little girl's face. She began to bring her love to Becky, as she called her, by talking to her, telling her that she understood the pain and the fear. She knew Becky had carried those memories for many years, and she felt deep compassion for the little girl. She was able to make the journey in her mind to embrace and hold Becky as she held the child to her heart and softly told the child of her love for her. She held Becky for a long time, deepening her feelings of love. She then asked Becky how she was feeling. As Rebecca allowed herself to be aware of Becky's feelings, she felt peace where she had felt fear and insecurity.

Rebecca was doing what we have been talking about in different forms with Freeze-Frame, Cut-Thru, and in feeling appreciation and care. She had shifted to the frequency of love in her heart and brought that love to the situation in her life. For Rebecca it was a memory of hurt. She did not need to remember it to bring the love there. She could have brought the transforming power of love into her feelings without the conscious memory. One way is not better or worse, just different. It is often easier and more efficient not to have to remember and get involved in the memories. For some people, there are times when it is easier to remember and then bring their love to that part of themselves. The important thing is to love. Don't get wrapped up in the drama. Everyone has drama. The drama is not important—the love is.

The outer expression of this change in Rebecca's life took place over a longer period of time. She began to find ways to acknowledge herself at work and eventually made changes that gave her much deeper satisfaction. This change also expressed itself as a renewed harmony in her marriage and her family life.

SENDING LOVE TO OTHERS

This is the fun part! Several days ago I was talking to a friend who had been a Baptist minister and a successful businessman. He told me that of all things he had learned in his life, sending love to others was for him the most important and meaningful.

There are so many people we can bless through the power of our love. We often find ourselves desiring to pray for or send love to someone during times of crisis in their lives—illness, divorce, jail, or loss. At that point we are aware that they really do need support. Love is a powerful support to them in their transformation, and sending it is a blessing to our lives as well.

Sending love is easy.

1. Bring that person into your mind. Think of their face or name.
2. Then think of the things you appreciate about them. Dwell on the positive qualities of that person's life. Feel your appreciation or care for them. As these loving feelings are in your heart, they are carrying your love to that person. Instead of appreciation, you may feel care, compassion, or love for the person.
3. Now allow yourself to deepen your feeling of love, as though you can connect directly with their heart and their soul. If you have an image of the person in your mind, you may actually be able to feel the flow of love from your heart. Sometimes I have had a sense of the person looking up and smiling at me, acknowledging and receiving that love. Stay with that deep, beautiful feeling—it is blessing you both.
4. When you release your focus upon them, allow yourself to acknowledge that the transformation being sought by their soul is taking place. Give thanks.

THE BOTTOM LINE—LIVING IN YOUR HEART

Having studied these powerful Universal Laws, it is easy to understand the effectiveness of the simple act of living from your heart. When you are centered in your heart, all of the Laws of Cause and Effect are operating to bring you love and wisdom in support of your life. The Law of Love is transforming; it uplifts your experiences, bringing forth fulfillment and meaning into your life.

You deserve the fun, the joy, the freedom, and the pure goodness that flows through the experience of the love that indwells you. The laws bring you this opportunity. The choice is yours.

"Is this all I have to do? Just live in my heart?" Basically that's it. It is that simple. The only problem is that we don't always remember. However, enlightenment is a matter of ratios. Today maybe you made it into your heart for thirty percent of the time. That is probably a pretty good inprovement from a year or two ago. With six months of sincere effort, maybe it will be forty-five percent. Wow, what a difference that would make in your life!

Think what life could be like in two years if you sought to live in your heart through those years. What possibilities await you!

THE FINAL QUESTION

If you aren't sure about all of this—all these laws and the way they operate—just go to your heart and put your question in that neutral space. That's a fun thing to do and you have allowed yourself to consider the possibility that there is order to life after all. See what your heart says!

Chapter 6

The Law of Giving

The Law of Giving—"True giving manifests love."

True giving is a free and natural response that takes place when we are in attunement with our spiritual nature. When our mind is receptive to that part of ourselves, we become channels for the expression of that spiritual presence, whether that expression is in giving to ourselves or giving to another. Our thoughts, feelings, and actions carry the nature of the Divine. This results in love flowing through us without thought of reward. This is true giving which according to another Law of Transformation, the Law of Giving, manifests love. True giving has been described as giving freely, giving without thought of return or reward. Edgar Cayce describes it this way:

> *That is the law of love.* Giving in action, without the force felt, expressed, manifested, shown, desired or reward for that given. (3744-5)

True giving is not a matter of what the outer action is, rather it is dependent on the inner focus. If the focus is on what I am going to get rather than what the other person will receive, then the giving is not filled with love and is not transformative. I experienced the difference in that focus just the other day.

A FOCUS ON CARE

It was one of those mornings. Everyone was running late, homework was lost, and shoes had disappeared. I was driving my children the mile from our house to the highway to catch the school bus. We arrived after the bus had pulled away. I started feeling frustrated. I had to take the time on an already busy morning to drive twenty minutes to the children's school and return. As I felt myself becoming increasingly tense and stressed, I realized my attention was all on me and my inconvenience. This was also an important experience for my children, so I reasoned I should bring them into the equation. We were right in the middle of a situation where our consequences were obvious. It appeared to be a very effective moment to examine what we had done wrong so this would not happen again. However, I had been working with this love concept long enough to check and make sure I was responding from the love in my heart before I began our dialogue.

I switched my attention to my heart through the technique Freeze-Frame. To activate the heart feeling in step three, I used sincere appreciation. As I began to appreciate my two wonderful children who do make it to the bus on most mornings, I felt myself relaxing and releasing the tension that had been building in my body. Nothing outwardly had changed—I was still sitting behind the wheel of my car, starting an unexpected trip, but the world I was perceiving had altered and with that change of perception came not only relaxation but also renewed feelings of serenity and energy.

When I asked my heart for my most effective response to this situation, the answer was very different than I had anticipated. I became aware of and understood the tension the children were under and the very demanding day they had ahead. It appeared far more efficient to support them in starting the rest of their day harmoniously than in rehashing a morning scenario in which we all already knew our mistakes. So as we drove to school, I put on some music and the children began to relax from our hectic morning with its unsuccessful rush for the bus. They arrived refreshed and renewed, ready to greet their classmates. I noticed that the sun was breaking through the clouds, making beautiful patterns on the redwood trees on either side of the road—more to appreciate! I returned home feeling peaceful, happy, and energized, rather than depleted and irritated as I would have been if I had chosen to stay in my state of frustration because of the inconvenience to me and had carried on in a corrective dialogue with two stressed children.

It was easy to recognize that switching to giving genuine care to my children from my heart, instead of expressing my selfish reactive response, brought physiological, mental, and emotional changes. These changes resulted not only in the pleasant feelings that added a greater quality to that experience, but they also resulted in an expanded wisdom that assisted the transformation of an experience from one of stress to one of regeneration.

CHANGE FOR OTHERS

The true giving referred to by the Law of Giving is unconditional. For instance, I care about you whether you care about me or not. I love you the way you are. I give my love to you freely whether or not you change.

There are times when we want to change someone because we love them. We frequently recognize self-destructive patterns in those we love. Because we care about them, we do not want to see them bring hurt and pain upon themselves. It is a natural response of our love to want to support someone in moving from hurtful patterns to healthy ones, to eliminate hurt, or to bring out the best in someone. However, it is seldom loving to manipulate others into making the changes we have decided are best for them.

How do we love without manipulation? We can use the Law of Giving and give freely to manifest the transforming power of love. It is this kind of giving that we see demonstrated every day as parents give love to their children. When a child who is hurt comes to you, your natural love response is to hold them and allow your feelings of love to flow to them. You love them in their hurt, just the way they are. It doesn't matter if they were right or wrong in what happened. In that true giving we have dropped the judgmental attitudes that separate us from the love we can express through our hearts. We then have access to its wisdom and its transformative power.

Once Victoria found little Vicki, her attention shifted from the change she was seeking as an adult to Little Vicki's need to be loved and accepted. Her attention shifted from getting to giving. Because that shift of attention was complete, little Vicki did not feel the rejection of manipulation and could accept the love she needed to transform the hurt she carried. The change of attention is from getting to giving. The Law of Giving is invoked by heartfelt caring. As a pure state, unconditional giving is very challenging to attain. If we had to attain it to be transformed, we would probably all give up trying. Fortunately, the Law of Giving operates to whatever extent our giving is unconditional. It's a ratio game. If our giving is ten percent unconditional, then ten percent of our giving manifests love. You have had relationships that have gone way beyond ten percent. In those relationships every degree of pure giving that you achieved released more of your love's transformative power. Even though you may have some ulterior motives for your love, the part of the giving that is unconditional manifests love to that degree. To whatever extent you freely give from the heart, that giving manifests love, and love transforms.

OVERCARE

I have found one very effective way to understand when the renewing flow of spirit is moving through my being and expressing in my actions, as opposed to when I have changed from true giving and attached conscious or subconscious conditions to my giving. I examine my experience in terms of care and overcare. Care is my genuine heart response of feeling care for or about another person. Care is renewing; it gives us energy. When we express genuine care for another, we feel invigorated and renewed. Overcare is a term developed by Childre to describe the kind of care that drains us. In his book *CUT-THRU* he shares an insight into his discovery of this balance.[1]

> In examining my own life a number of years ago, I realized that in caring for people, I would frequently worry about them, wonder if they were okay, and get upset if their problems kept growing in spite of my efforts to help them. I became anxious and concerned. Why? "Because I care," I told myself. Yet it puzzled me that my caring effort kept draining me. I felt I was carrying the world on my back and wondered, "Is it worth it?"
>
> In studying this enigma, it became obvious to me that I was caring too much about nonessentials. And on important matters, I was taking care over a line and into stress. I realized I wasn't alone. That's what most people do. I de-

cided to research this type of stress-producing care and coined it "overcare." Overcare is care that becomes a drain or deficit in the human system, offering no sight of any real solution to a problem. It takes you out of "flow." When you overcare about what you love, care about, feel compassion for, or appreciate, the stress that is produced generates incoherent frequencies in the electrical system of the heart, and that incoherence is communicated to the brain and every cell in the body. When people keep worrying about the things they care about, they dig themselves into a pit of endless anxiety. Overcare always spawns stress. The world has become stagnant from overcare and the result is a widespread feeling of "no hope."

Often, when we overcare, our caring is excessive or tied into a perception of "should" or "have to." Or maybe we have added thoughts of "what if," "what will they think," resentments of the time spent, or other worries to our response of feeling care. With overcare, we lose energy. We are not renewed; rather, we are drained. It is usually overcare that leads us into the experience of burnout. Because of overcare, we may find ourselves resenting our jobs or our families.

BURNOUT

I got my first professional case of burnout after being a minister for four years. I had a small church in Montana. Because the church was so small and because I didn't know any better, I kept doing everything I could think of to make it grow. I wanted to really care for the people of the church, so I taught many classes and had many activities. I was there for everything that went on, which was most days of the week, and commuted an hour each way every day to do these things.

One day someone canceled a counseling appointment, and I found that I felt relieved. Later that week I was waiting for a class to start, and I found myself hoping no one came. When I recognized this feeling, I stopped and began to check out other areas of activity. I realized that I was dreading Sunday morning. I didn't have anything new, interesting, insightful, entertaining, or profound to say. What I wanted to do was sleep in. It wasn't winter anymore, but I wished for a good Montana blizzard to get me off the hook for the Sunday service. The church was in the process of buying a new (to us) building to meet in. We had been through months of meetings—yes or no, for or against. In the end, everyone had supported the move, but the process of examining all the repercussions and advantages had been exhausting.

I was burned out. I had gone from feeling great care for the people of the church and for our work to not caring. Fortunately, the church board and members were very understanding and supported my taking several months of leave while they cared for the church and moved us into the new building.

During my renewal time, I watched my four-year-old son. He had combined several characters including a cowboy, Mickey Mouse, and Superman into a persona he would call Super Mickey. He put on a cape, cowboy hat, mask, and toy six shooters and became an invincible, all-powerful champion of the good. He would then run across the room calling, "Here comes Super Mickeeeeeey," and leap up in the air, landing in an invincible pose. Every now and then, the landing would not go so well and a skinned knee would result. In those moments he became Peter again and needed his mother or father to hold him for a second while the hurt went away so he could return to invincibility. I realized that both of us had been playing Super Mickey; he as a four year old and I as an adult.

I returned from my time of renewal to find the church well and strong and to discover that I again could feel my true care for the people. I enjoyed many happy, satisfying years there. However, I watched my energy expenditures as a minister to avoid further burnout. As diligently as I tried to understand my experience, it wasn't until I heard the concept of overcare explained many years later at the Institute of HeartMath that I saw the whole picture of the energy drain that I experienced. I knew the idea that I had simply worked too many hours was not an accurate understanding of what had occurred. Often my extra hours had been energy producing. It was the "going the extra mile" or that additional giving that was a real add-on to my day. The inner perceptions that I held were the difference between the Law of Giving being activated by my "true giving" or overcare draining my energy.

The simple understanding of the difference between true care and overcare is that true care is energy producing and overcare is energy reducing. Our heartfelt response to the opportunity to support another is one of the healthiest things we can do for ourselves. However, when our response is one of obligation, "should," "have to," "what will they think if I don't," or substituting worry for care, we lose our energy and end up fatigued. True care is another way of expressing true giving with its resultant flow of spiritual energy through the heart.

We are looking at the effective utilization of spiritual energy. When spiritual energy is received into the system, we can short it out and block its flow or use it effectively. The feeling of care sets up the receptive mechanism and overcare blocks it. Let's examine how some of this looks at a third-dimensional level.

SCIENCE OF CARE

In a previous chapter we looked at the phenomenon of entrainment in which the separate oscillating systems of the body came into highly efficient synchronization with each other when the heartfelt feeling of appreciation was generated (see fig. 3B). The feeling of care has similar results. The body responds with this more efficient level of operation. We also know that we feel good. The result of feeling care is physiological efficiency, balance, and harmonious feelings.

From the frustration graph we also know that frustrated feelings produce the opposite effect (see fig. 3A). When our care becomes worry or frustration, the systems of our body are out of sync, and we feel the drain of inefficient use of our energy on all levels. No wonder we end up fatigued and over time we burn out.

Care is that true giving without our mind attaching conditions such as what the results should be or what the response to us should be. It is an expression of loving unconditionally. The worry and frustration are the results of "hand-me-down" patterns we learned from the way we saw someone else care. We are involved in the conditions—the person getting well, doing the right thing, or liking us for our effort. Worry and frustration are not care. They are identity with our expectations and a sure path to burnout.

CAN LOVE SAY NO?

As I have sought to understand unconditional love and share that love with others, I have found many questions, both from myself and others, that are a legitimate part of our experience of learning how to give love.

One of the most frequently asked questions is: If I am loving unconditionally, do I have to do whatever the person asks? Is that the kind of giving that is unconditional? Perhaps it is easiest to understand this question when thinking of a parent's love for a child. There are many things we might like to get the child, but we realize that not every candy in the store—not everything the child wants—is something that love would give. Love would strike a balance that supported the child's growth and development. Sometimes that might be a treat or a toy; other times those things would be denied. How does one know which to do in love? I do not believe there are outer rules that can provide that answer. The answer comes as a result of our love itself.

When we feel love or care for another, we activate the intuitive intelligence of the heart. That intelligence knows what is right for both of us. When we access that intelligence through our love, we know when we need to say no or yes to something as an act of love. This is the giving that invokes the Law of Giving—giving from both the intelligence and the care of the heart. It is through the heart that we become the expression of our spiritual nature and its transformative power.

Unconditional love accepts a person as he or she is, warts and all. It is not unconditional love to pretend that an alcoholic is not an alcoholic, or that a violent person is not violent, or that a part of ourselves that is violent or angry is not that way. Unconditional love accepts and loves others as they are. It does not pretend that they are different than they are or that their desires are either healthy or wise. We can refuse the alcoholic a drink and keep out of the way of a violent person when such people are being violent and still love them unconditionally. Judging by the outer action, one may appear to be withholding, but viewed from the inner perspective one can see the giving of love as intuitive support. This is true giving. The outer form of response does not activate the Law of Giving—that comes from the inner response of one's love.

LOVE AS COURAGE

We have probably all seen thousands of greeting cards with syrupy phrases about love. These tend to leave us with an impression of love as soft, sweet, and not appropriate for the hard demands of life. However, the heart is the source of courage, and no courage is greater than that inspired by love. People have again and again faced great difficulty and danger to care for the ones they love. Often when we seek guidance from the heart, we hear a very demanding courageous instruction for our lives to take on the hard questions and put our love into action. I remember receiving such an instruction from my heart in dealing with a friend whom I suspected of being an alcoholic.

My friend's behavior was suspicious. Out of sincere care for him, I had to investigate. As the pieces came together, my heart kept pushing me toward a confrontation. It also told me to get good help so that the confrontation could be effective. With others who cared about this man, we held an intervention where we confronted him with his behavior, its effects on us, and a ride to a treatment facility. We knew of his financial needs and had made arrangements for these—his house, etc. He wanted to leave the minute he discovered what was going on, but we didn't let him until we had expressed ourselves. He accepted the ride to be evaluated, entered treatment, and has now been sober for many years. It was one of the most difficult things many of us in that room had ever done. However, it was the expression of our love.

In the above situation unconditional love demanded that we commit to love our friend regardless of whether or not our intervention was successful. The boundaries we committed ourselves to set when his drinking affected our lives were firm. However, even in enforcing those boundaries, we would have needed to do so out of our love for him, rather than our frustration or judgment of his behavior. Many people have gone through similar confrontations with friends and family members who exhibit destructive behavior without the successful outcome we were fortunate to experience. Their challenge has been to continue loving yet deal directly with that which was destructive to their lives.

Was our confrontation of the alcoholic considered manipulation? Yes, it was manipulation. That is why it was so important to check that what we are responding to is the wisdom from our hearts. It has never appeared possible to me to put rules around what love is and isn't. With every rule I have tried to set, I have found an exception. What becomes important is getting past all the ideas in our heads and finding the direction from the wisdom of our heart. Through the sincerity of our love and care we can access that wisdom. It is there—in our hearts—that we touch the infinite intelligence of the Divine expressing personally in our lives. Chapter 8 on wisdom has some techniques to help people connect with that guidance.

GIVING TO SELF

If true giving is focused on the other person, instead of us, what about our needs? Is it ever true giving to give to ourselves or to think of our interests? That is a question that I have heard frequently from people working with the many Cayce readings in which Edgar Cayce told people "others, not self."

In my understanding of Cayce's work, he gave this admonition to help us release much of the "me and mine" that is rampant in the human species. Yet he often counseled people to take care of themselves. In fact, he often instructed them on self-care. He gave thousands of physical readings assisting people in taking loving care of themselves. When the attitude is simply toward getting something for one's self, it is often motivated by a feeling of lack rather than love. However, giving to oneself in love is as much an expression of true giving as giving to another. I have often appreciated and benefited from those who gave themselves a good education when I learned from their knowledge, or from those who gave themselves the gift of beauty as I enjoyed the serenity of their home, art, or garden.

Don't violate another Universal Law when applying this one. As a simple analogy: don't overload the boat. The law of gravity will overpower the law of flotation if proper balance is not obtained. Likewise in applying the Golden Rule, don't neglect yourself in favor of another.

The Law of Equality—"Your true needs, wants, desires, hopes, dreams, wishes, and their fulfillment are as important as those of any other soul in existence."[2]

This law emphasizes that you should consider yourself not higher, not lower, but equal to others and treat yourself in that way. One Cayce reading explains why this is so:

. . . the care of each soul, each individual, is just as necessary—[as that of any other] because each is just as precious as the other in the sight of the Creative Force or God. (4047-2)

The criteria is not outer, but inner. If we turn to our heart wisdom, we do find many ways of giving to ourselves, some in material ways, some in other ways. It is the wisdom of the heart that is quickened by our love and which is expressed as care or self-appreciation that allows us to see clearly whether an action for ourselves is the giving of love or the desires of our insecurities.

DEEP HEART LISTENING

The Law of Giving requires true giving, which comes from the heart. In interpersonal communication, I have been aware of the difference between an intellectual concept of giving and a heart experience of giving. Many people in our society have been taught the communication skill of reflective listening. In the reflective listening exercise, the listener attempts to clearly hear the message and reflects back to the speaker the content of both the thoughts and feelings that the listener is expressing. It is a very helpful model for clarifying communication. I have seen some of these communications go beyond clarified messages to new levels of transformed understandings or to a new depth of relationship for those involved. What takes these communications to the level of transformation? Let's examine these techniques in terms of the Law of Giving.

When the listener is focusing his or her attention on the person's statement, that is a giving—a giving of attention. When the listener is reflecting the content, that is a giving of acknowledgment. What does it take for these communications to move from a giving to a "true giving"—thus activating the transformative power of the Law of Giving? My perception is that when the listener stays focused in the head, trying to remember and analyze in order to accurately reflect the information, a limited form of communication may occur, but transformation does not. The focus for the listener is on the listener's performance rather than on the speaker.

At times another dynamic has taken place. The listeners focus on caring about the speakers. Their feelings of genuine care focus their energy in their hearts rather than their heads. Regardless of whether or not they can accurately reflect the literal content of the message, they receive and acknowledge the essence of the message. This approach transforms the experience from a message exchange into a deep experience of understanding between people. The entire nature of the communication changes and transformation takes place in the exchange.

In a recent meeting at work, we were discussing our various

goals. My friend Jean, seated beside me, presented some options she was exploring in accomplishing her goals. Rachel, who was seated across from her, responded, "You aren't having any fun in your work!" Jean thought for a moment, then acknowledged that was true. I realized how deeply Rachel had heard Jean, who had been talking on a different subject. Rachel's response not only acknowledged a deep understanding of Jean's statement, beyond the thoughts and feelings involved, but it also changed our discussion from an outer focus to an inner one from which we could bring a new dynamic to all of our activities. Rachael had really cared about Jean and part of her giving was her care as she listened from her heart. Because of the love carried through her giving, we were all changed.

The true giving in this situation comes from the heartfelt desire to understand—to listen deeply. It is care about the other person. The care puts the listener's energy in his or her heart rather than in the head, and the giving of attention and acknowledgment becomes a true giving. The love that is manifest in that experience transforms the understanding and the relationship.

Does this mean we can fix soured relationships by listening for a few moments from the heart? No, that is not what the law says. It does mean that the heart desire to really understand the other person can help us begin to bring real transformative power into the relationship. With that present, we can begin to understand and care about each other, key elements to a healthy relationship.

One of the greatest gifts you will discover from using the Laws of Love and Giving is the experience of joy. With every experience of giving in love—true giving—joy and fulfillment grow.

We have explored the Law of Love and the Law of Giving, which is a specific application of the Law of Love. The next law, called the "Whole Law," is also a specific application of the Law of Love. Edgar Cayce describes this as the law that stands out above all others.

**The Whole Law—"You shall love the
Lord your God with all your heart, your mind,
your body; and your neighbor as your self."**

THE WHOLE TEACHING

The Edgar Cayce readings unequivocally describe the Whole

Law as the whole purpose of our experience, the whole reason for our being here. They even strikingly describe it as the whole answer to the world conditions, the whole answer to each and every soul. What is this amazing law?

> You shall love the Lord your God with all your heart, your mind, your body; your neighbor as yourself. This as He gave is the whole law. There is none above that. (1348-1)AR

The all-inclusive nature of this law is evident from these statements:

> This is the whole law—the spiritual law, the mental law, the material law. (1662-1)

> This is the whole will of the Father to His children. The rest of that recorded in Holy Writ . . . is merely the attempt to explain, to analyze, to justify or to meet that saying, that truth . . . (2524-3)

Such dramatic statements invite us to fully examine this teaching so that we may understand and apply it. Note I have called this a teaching—it is not a law, for in the way in which it is stated it can be broken. You may, for example, hate your neighbor which is contrary to [breaks] the teaching.

Cayce's source has termed the teaching a law to give it more emphasis. Although it is not a law, it is in fact an excellent teaching on how to apply the Law of Love. When you are teaching someone to love the Lord your God with all your heart, your mind, your body, and your neighbor as yourself, you are giving to them a great key to applying the Law of Love which is: love transforms. To be consistent with our definition of a Universal Law, I will not refer to this further as a law but rather as the Whole Teaching.

Jesus, too, strongly emphasized this Whole Teaching, calling it a commandment of the law in this interesting exchange with the Pharisees who were concerned with Jewish religious law:

> Hearing that Jesus had silenced the Sadducees, the Pharisees got together. One of them, an expert in the law, tested him with this question: "Teacher, which is the greatest commandment in the Law?"

Jesus replied, " 'Love the Lord your God with all your heart and with all your soul and with all your mind.' This is the first and greatest commandment. And the second is like it: 'Love your neighbor as yourself.' All the Law and the Prophets hangs on these two commandments." Matthew 22:34-40 (NIV)

As we further explore the Universal Laws, you may begin to wonder if you can ever work with all of them, or even just remember them. The Whole Teaching is the key to all the Universal Laws. If you can truly know this lawful teaching and fully live it in your life, you will be fulfilling all the Universal Laws in the highest way.

APPLYING THE WHOLE TEACHING

This Whole Teaching expresses in one statement the basic relationship required among the infinite presence, myself as an entity in the earth, and my neighbor. It shows the need for balance in loving—in loving the Presence in me, in loving *all* that I am just as I am, and in loving all that my neighbor is, just as he/she is. Since love is in infinite supply, the ultimate—the ideal—is to love each of these three with all my heart, mind, and body. This needs to be done within the context of my everyday life, where I am—in my actions, reactions, and interactions with those with whom I associate.

For greater understanding, let's consider separately the two basic portions of the Whole Teaching.

"Love the Lord your God with all your heart, your mind, your body."

What does this really mean and how can we go about doing it? If we love someone "with all our heart, our mind, our body," obviously we would be devoted to that person and our thoughts and actions would be related to and influenced by that person. For example, Brother Lawrence in the classic, *Practice of the Presence of God,* writes of his conviction that every task he did, no matter how menial, even to washing the pots and pans, he did for God and with the thought of God.[3]

In my own life, I have found simple ways to connect with my love of God. The first is a deep feeling of gratitude in my heart for the amazing creation I am—from the external one to the internal one. The second is appreciating the love God expresses for me through the wonderful people and experiences with which He has filled my life.

Cayce's readings give the following two criteria for loving God:
- We love God by loving others.
- We love God by loving ourselves (our own unique individuality).

Therefore, the first half of the teaching, loving God, is fulfilled by the second half, loving self and others.

LOVE YOUR NEIGHBOR AS YOURSELF

Who is this neighbor we need to learn to love? The readings repeatedly point out that this neighbor includes: your brother, your sister, your friend, your foe, your enemies, those who would do you harm, those who would abuse you, or those who would use you. In so doing (loving them), you create through the Creative Forces the ability to overcome difficulties in your own life. Your life becomes more meaningful and thereby gives hope to others.

How can you love the difficult characters? By giving day by day, little by little, words and acts that exemplify that you do love that person in the same manner or way that you love yourself. From our normal perceptions of difficult individuals, that is not easy. That is why the instruction begins with "love." When you focus your attention in the heart, find just one thing to appreciate about that person and sincerely feel it, you find your perceptions shift as your heart intelligence assists you. As this happens, day by day, your feeling and perceptions of love and understanding will grow.

The above clearly requires that we accept our neighbor just as he or she is for we cannot love that person if we are busy finding fault, feeling superior, judging, condemning, or criticizing. When we are judging another person, we are blocking our own wisdom which can instruct us on how to most effectively relate to or understand that individual. Our judgmental attitude cuts off the connection with the heart, whereas our intuitive intelligence gives us the wisdom to relate effectively. As the result of our judgmental attitude, we find ourselves in an internal state that is not pleasant, a state of internal isolation and external inefficiency. The way out lies in loving another unconditionally—that is without any ifs, ands, or buts. That is a tall order, unless we can engage the wisdom of our hearts to help us out.

LEARNING TO LOVE FRED

I remember Fred, a difficult individual in my church who frustrated me. He seemed never to listen, but always took off on some strange opinion of his own which seemed irrelevant to what the group was discussing. I decided to try to appreciate him. The next time our board met, he attended our meeting. A vacancy had occurred on the board, and someone had suggested he fill it. Knowing that I had just set up my greatest challenge, I didn't object. Now I would have to love him or I would really be putting myself in an unpleasant situation. At each meeting I focused on one thing I could appreciate about him. I already knew what I didn't like about him so I did not need to focus on that. By the end of six months, he and I were going for coffee together. I began to enjoy his company. His ideas never did end up being very relevant to our topics, but I found in him a sincerity and a willingness to help others and to serve selflessly that were exceptional. I enjoyed our friendship for many years.

The teaching requires that we love our neighbor just as we love ourselves. If we don't love ourselves very much, it can be very difficult to love a neighbor more, for love comes from within. When I looked at why Fred's habit of switching to irrelevant topics irritated me so, I realized that when I was in the early part of my legal career, I was a poor speaker who would wander as I was trying to make points. It took great self-discipline to overcome that tendency, and I controlled myself with a strong judgment on that type of behavior. As I learned to appreciate Fred for who he was, I was also able to love myself and release the judgment I had placed on myself. The more we learn to drop conditions we have placed on loving our neighbors, the easier we will find it to drop conditions placed on loving ourselves.

Know that the fault you find in others is a reflection of a fault in yourself. Be to others just as you would have others be to you, and you will remove much of that. (1688-9)AR

Our sincerity of purpose, our desire to put the Whole Teaching into effect in our activities greatly impacts our growth in love. If we seek to manifest love by utilizing our inherent abilities to serve others in whatever we are doing, we find the greatest opportunity for development, for then we are giving expression to our love for our neighbors and ourselves.

Chapter 7

Freedom Through Forgiveness

For hatred does not cease by hatred at any time;
hatred ceases by love . . .

Dhammapada[1]

. . . It is in forgiving that we are forgiven . . .

Saint Francis of Assisi

The Law of Forgiveness— "Forgiveness heals and empowers the one who forgives."

The Law of Forgiveness, another of the great Laws of Transformation, offers us the gift of the freedom to be who we really are. It is a specific application of the Law of Love and is deeply transformative in its effect on our lives.

Many of the limiting patterns we experience in our daily lives are the results of our interactions with other people. Because we have not learned to know ourselves as the powerful spiritual beings we truly are, we find ourselves hurt by others. Our response to this hurt is to develop the perception of ourselves as powerless and subject to hurt by others. To protect ourselves against the perceived power of others, we associate our hurt with them and hold resentment against them. The holding of resentment is so contrary to our true spiritual nature that it becomes a very destructive force within us. Part of the reason for this is that all resentment includes resentment of oneself.

While we may direct our resentment toward another, our own perceived powerlessness is a large part of what we actually resent. The Law of Attraction brings reflections of this resentment into manifestation in our lives. We keep facing the problem created by our resentment. The healing of that resentment, whether at the mental or physical level of expression, is through the process of forgiveness. When that forgiveness takes place, the manifestations of the resentment within our body are free to be healed, and we experience the return of our personal power. Forgiveness brings us freedom from those perceptions that enslave and limit us. Free of these limiting perceptions, we can be who we really are.

Cayce's source assures us that forgiveness is important as we try to manifest the purpose written upon our hearts:

> For, inasmuch as you may forgive or forget past hurts or the like, the greater may be the ability to fulfill the purposes for which the entity came into the earth at this particular period. (3180-2)AR

EDWENE GAINES—CANCER HEALED

Edwene Gaines is one of the outstanding prosperity teachers of our time. In her workshop, "Prosperity Plus," she shares the following experience as the way she discovered the need for and the power of forgiveness.

Edwene was six months pregnant when her husband took all their money and abandoned her in the city of Hong Kong. Having no resources and being in an advanced state of pregnancy, she had to find work in a foreign country where she knew no one, in order to get enough money to live on and eventually get home. Part of the energy that drove her and motivated her for many years was her anger, resentment, and hatred toward her ex-husband. Some years later she developed cancer, and the doctors told her there was nothing they or she could do. She should make out a will because in six months or less she would be dead.

Edwene had become a student of spiritual laws and now recognized that the cancer was a manifestation of her hatred for her ex-husband. Her hatred was, as all resentment, not killing the one toward whom she directed it but was instead killing the one who carried it. She had to find a way to forgive him. Through diligent seeking and earnest effort she did come to a point of forgiveness, and her cancer was totally healed. From her healing and her growth in connection with her own true self, Edwene went on to fulfill her purpose of supporting and inspiring many thousands of people and helping them to know and connect with their own inner wisdom and to be about the purposes of their lives. Forgiveness heals and empowers the one who forgives.

WHAT IS FORGIVENESS?

Forgiveness is the removal of the inner blocks we hold that are barriers to loving another or ourselves. It is also sending love freely to the one we have judged as wrong. Forgiveness is not a neutral state of indifference. It is a positive, powerful state of love. It is achieved by calling on the divine presence within us, acting with its assistance to dissolve the barrier of resentment, and then sending the love to the one we resented.

Many people are afraid to forgive because they feel they must remember the wrong or they will not learn from it. The opposite is true. Through forgiveness, the wrong is released from its emotional stranglehold on us so that we can learn from it. Through the power and intelligence of the heart, the release of forgiveness brings expanded intelligence to work with the situation more effectively. The tragedy of unforgiveness is that individuals continue to inflict hurt upon themselves when the event could be over—while denying themselves the true wisdom they could gain from their experience.

Forgiveness heals and empowers the one who forgives. This law, the Law of Forgiveness, deals not only with physical healing but also with the return to a state of wholeness within ourselves. It operates to restore the power we have given away. We return not only to connection with our true power but also, more important, to the connection with our true self.

REBECCA

In chapter 5, "How to Love," I described a part of the experience of Rebecca who had suffered abuse from an uncle. Rebecca also worked on the experience of forgiving her uncle. She realized that her resentment toward him was only hurting herself. She wanted to be free of those feelings. The first step in the healing of that resentment was giving love to herself.

It is important to recognize that when someone else had hurt us, we can sometimes jump to forgiveness too quickly. Resentment is a way we try to remember to protect ourselves from hurt by others. It is not effective for us, because we have a fully developed wisdom in the mind and heart to do that effectively. However, there is often a preliminary step before we are ready to forgive.

Because forgiveness is sending love and understanding to our wrongdoer, it is difficult to immediately forgive. The part of us that is hurt doesn't want to do that because we want that love for ourselves. We need that love to heal our own pain. Rebecca moved to forgiveness by using her love to heal that part of herself that carried the pain. This is the first step of forgiveness.

After Rebecca had several times gone within to the memory of herself as Becky the hurt child and felt the peace and release from fear that was brought by her love, she was able to turn her inner attention to her uncle. As she felt whole, strong, and at peace, she brought his memory to mind and saw him as a person who was ill, controlled by a disease that made him act in violation of himself and others. She felt the power that she now had, having overcome his actions and mastered her own mental, emotional energy.

Feeling powerful in her own right, Rebecca had no difficulty in sending her love to her uncle. It started as her sense of compassion for him and developed into a sense of love for the person he really was, not the person controlled by alcoholism and drug-induced violence. She felt compassion for that person, but she also realized that he was a good and valuable person when he had the opportunity to express his real self.

With the sending of that love, Rebecca felt the surge of another level of inner freedom and power. She was free—free of the hurt that had affected her life for so long—and free of her uncle. Resentment no longer controlled her life. She had entered into a new experience of self-mastery.

Rebecca also felt a change within her body. For the first time she felt a physical change that she attributed to her body releasing the resentment. She understood that through her forgiveness she had healed herself mentally, emotionally, spiritually, and physically from the "dis-ease" she had carried in her system due to the resentment.

Let's review the steps that Rebecca went through in her forgiveness:

1. Healing of the mental/emotional hurt through loving herself.
2. Being aware of her own peace and strength from her self-
   love.
3. Remembering the person who wronged her.
4. Looking on him with compassion for the insanity of his
   disease. (Those who wrong another are insane, in violation
   of themselves, and blinded by their own hurt and pain.)
5. Focusing on his redeeming qualities and feeling appreciation for that aspect of his being.
6. Appreciating her power and peace while accepting the
   sense of freedom that her forgiveness brought her.

Rebecca had the opportunity to be present with her uncle a
year later through several steps of his dying process. She gained
a lot from the experience and had some good conversations with
him. She realized he was pained by the hurt he had brought to
others and she was able to express her forgiveness directly to
him. She described it as a very special moment in her life.

SELF-FORGIVENESS

Be not afraid because you have faltered anywhere. For
He has said, "I forgive, even as you forgive others." Then
how forgiving are you? Answer this, and you will know just
how you have been forgiven. It is the law, it is the Lord, it is
love. (3376-2)AR

The steps for self-forgiveness are the same as forgiveness of
others. It begins with love and acceptance for yourself. The action that you carry guilt about came out of your own dysfunc-
tionality, immaturity, and alienation from yourself. Because love
has the power to transform all patterns, all that we have done is
forgivable. Through the love within us, we all have the capability
of transforming and completely overcoming whatever we, in our
immaturity, have done to ourselves or another.

In 1971 I was working at the governor's office in Santa Fe,
New Mexico, as a law student proofing legislative bills. My wife
had called early in the day with a question about the teenage
boy we had taken into our home. He had not gone to school that

day. When I returned from lunch, the secretary asked me if I had gotten the message to call my wife. I told her that I did, assuming that she was talking about my wife's earlier call. When I got home my wife was not there. We were to discover later that the young man had ended my wife's life during that afternoon. On the pad next to the telephone was a message. It read, "Please call soon." I knew that message was for me. Had I not misunderstood the secretary's statement, my wife might still be alive.

I am very grateful for the Law of Forgiveness. I do not know what alternatives might have existed for that day. But I do know that it took a lot of love for me to find the freedom of self-forgiveness. Compassion for ourselves is so important because we do make mistakes that hurt others. Some are far beyond any ability we may have to make amends. I am sure my desire to forgive the young man who took her life was a part of my forgiveness for myself. Love does not judge us; we do that to ourselves. We can choose to accept that love for ourselves and be free.

Some of us carry some big mistakes, some carry smaller ones. Some of the things we often feel most guilty about are tied to patterns of shame within us and aren't even hurtful to others. Forgiveness frees us of all of it. Bring that love to yourself and heal your own hurt. Then understand your own dysfunction and have compassion for yourself—you would if it were someone else! Then just love you. Appreciate all the things you do right, the steps you have made, the blessings that you still have, the opportunity to give to life. Enjoy that powerful flow of love from your heart. You are a being of love. Be at peace.

PATIENCE, PERSEVERANCE, CONNECTION

The Law of Forgiveness was one of the major teachings of Jesus. Many have spoken it in the Lord's Prayer: "Forgive us our debts as we forgive our debtors." In His teaching on how long we work with forgiveness, Jesus showed His understanding of the Universal Laws of Attraction and Forgiveness. Recognizing that whatever we draw to us is within ourselves, He answered Peter's question, " 'Lord, how often shall my brother sin against me, and I forgive him? As many as seven times?' Jesus said to him, 'I do not say to you seven times, but seventy times seven.'" (Matthew 18:21, 22 RSV)

Because the outer is a reflection of what we are holding inside, the work of transforming the inner pattern of resentment is not over until it is totally healed, even if we have to work with it many times. Once healed, it will not manifest again in the outer; instead, the love experienced within will show itself in our world.

This process is illustrated in the diagram below. Focusing our attention inward on the core heart feelings connects us with our own spirit, our connection to the infinite presence of God. The divine presence as higher intelligence and transformative power then moves from the center of our being, out through the levels of our mental and emotional system, transforming the limiting patterns contained there.

Diagram of Our Journey of Awareness

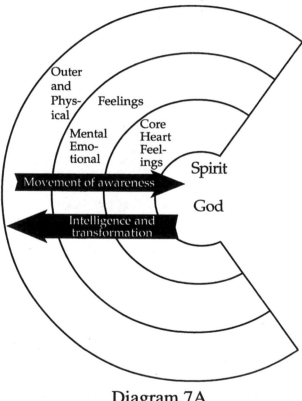

Diagram 7A

Fig. 7A. The inner journey diagramed here is a journey of awareness. By connecting with the heart feelings such as love, you connect with your own spirit, releasing the greater power of the indwelling divine presence into the mental and emotional levels of yourself.

Central to the experience of forgiveness is the movement of our attention from the outer condition of our lives, past the mental and emotional levels where we store the limiting patterns we are projecting out into our lives, and finally through the heart feelings, focusing our attention on the divine presence or our own spiritual nature—the "Kingdom of God" in us. In this way our awareness becomes the vehicle in consciousness through which the wholeness and love of that Presence can manifest.

In its simplest form, all religions teach this movement of awareness as the process of prayer, meditation, or contemplation—the way to your heart. Many teachers and spiritual paths have given other specific techniques for accomplishing this inner connection with the spiritual self. These are very supportive of the successful experience of forgiveness. Yet forgiveness is also there for those who have not embraced such disciplines. Forgiveness is a frequency found in the heart. What is necessary is your own love and desire for your release.

PATTERNS AT BIRTH

The operation of the Universal Laws is most clearly seen when one is willing to patiently and honestly examine one's own life. While honest self-examination is never an easy task, understanding the Universal Laws greatly simplifies the process.

Understanding the events that affected childhood, where we acquired many of our mental and emotional patterns, is a very challenging part of our self-examination. It appears that an individual has not had the opportunity to create the situations he or she meets as a child. Understanding our relationship to our childhood experiences is often helpful in our forgiveness work, because much of what we discover we need to forgive is from that time.

We are usually unable to know the specific reason that a child is experiencing a difficulty. A part of the child's process can be understood through the knowledge of the laws. Through the Law of Choice, "Life is the experience of our choices," we know that the soul of the child has made the choice to transform a part of human consciousness through the experience of a particular condition. The process of transforming the limitations that humankind holds requires that those conditions be met and transformed within one's self in order to affect the consciousness of humankind. Each transformation by each individual dissolves the power of limited ideas over human consciousness and strengthens the patterns of wholeness.

We have seen examples of this in Jesus' overcoming the idea of death and in one alcoholic who has gotten sober supporting another in overcoming his addiction. Each overcoming brings a degree of freedom to us all.

The belief that the soul who entered into the life experience of a child may have been involved in giving or receiving such a condition in a prior experience in the earth is consistent with knowledge of the laws. This concept of prior life experiences in the earth is called reincarnation. Personal responsibility for the condition one enters at birth is called karma—the extension of the laws across lifetimes. The laws involved in bringing a seed sown in a past life to harvest in this are sometimes referred to as "karmic laws." Here, the user is generally referring to the Laws of Cause and Effect operating beyond one lifetime.

There are many reasons a soul may choose a difficult path of experience. It would be neither helpful nor accurate to assume the one-on-one return of the karmic laws to describe another's situation. Whether or not these concepts of personal responsibility are valid for any single individual's experience, it is true that by meeting this situation successfully, the person learns the wisdom that the soul is seeking to gain through the experience.

A child's environment also strongly impacts the life pattern a child experiences. As children, we have very receptive minds and we are strongly influenced by the mass consciousness of our family and our culture, both at birth and in the early years of our development. Some of those patterns we receive into our mind as our own. Some of these will be healthy patterns, and some will be unhealthy or immature patterns. As these patterns become a part of our life experience, we have the opportunity to become an active force in bringing a higher consciousness to these situations.

PURPOSE OF THE LAWS

One of the most important elements in understanding the operation of the Universal Laws is recognizing that there is an overall purpose to the life experience that all the workings of the Universal Laws serve. When Jesus was asked a question raised by the Laws of Cause and Effect or karma, He responded not by commenting on those laws themselves, but by pointing out their purpose. Let's look at that purpose.

The disciples asked Jesus whether a person's affliction was caused by a sin the person had committed or was it caused by his parents' sin. In other words, what was the cause that would lawfully result in that affliction? Jesus responded by saying the cause lay not in the errors made by the person, but rather "so that the work of God might be displayed in his life." (John 9:3 NIV) Jesus was acknowledging that the view we often get by focusing on the Universal Laws—that our actions are always the creative instruments—is not ultimately true. The laws serve the purpose of manifesting the works of God or giving expression to the Divine in us. This purpose is the real cause of what is created. The Universal Laws are the instruments of that purpose. It is through their operation that the purpose is accomplished.

As we look at causation and recognize that our actions build the next round of our experience, the view which appears is one of seeing a building as being built from the bottom up. The truth is that the divine purpose is the cause of our experience, just as the architect's image of the building is its cause. The building that results has already been specified and designed according to the structural principles and laws known to the architect. Constructing the building from the ground up is simply the process by which that creation is made manifest. However, the quality of construction is of vital importance in the resulting creation.

The Universal Laws are our principles of construction, and while they are important to know to make the work of construction easier and more efficient, the real creation of the building is a cocreative process we engage in with the Architect. It is His plan that is being materialized. Understanding that the purpose of all experience is to express the Divine within us allows us to work with these laws as a faithful contractor. We may lay our bricks one upon the other, but the design is already given and the result is His.

Remembering this purpose as we examine the Universal Laws and our applications of them in our own lives helps us to avoid the judgments of guilt, mistakes, and self-criticism. We relate to the plan of the architect and recognize that the laws are not to punish mistakes; rather, they are to help us release weak construction and discover that which is enduring, true, and brings forth the full manifestation of the divine plan. Our experience of limitations provides us the opportunity to recognize those limitations on our own, and in releasing them for a truer way, we give expression to the Divine within.

As humankind has evolved, generation after generation, experience after experience, we have met the creations of our past; and, gaining practice with them, we have lifted them, step by step, through what has often seemed a very slow process of acquiring wisdom and understanding of our creation and the creative process. To accomplish our purpose, we enter into our life experience so that we can transform the limiting patterns that are a part of ourselves and our society. A major portion of that work is through forgiveness by which we release past judgments. In this way we grow in our ability to express the divine presence within us as we live and work with the conditions of that life experience. The inner spiritual nature we will ultimately manifest is the work of God in us of which Jesus spoke.

We bring forth our indwelling love through entering into the pattern that we find in our lives and bringing about the transformation of that pattern through our own living experience. As we accomplish this individually, it not only changes our own life experience, but it also creates a healing effect in the collective process in which the pattern of transformation is now reinforced. All people who respond to a situation with love for those involved become models of transformation and provide for all others the supportive presence of their own transforming love.

Part of my own recognition of the validity of this understanding of the purpose for our life situations has come from talking to people who have faced and met the challenge of a pattern which was destructive to themselves and others. Once individuals have experienced transformation, they have again and again turned to me and said, "It was worth it." With the awareness and satisfaction they have gained in transforming these limitations, which have included every pain and difficulty I could have imagined, they have consistently said afterward that they were grateful for having undergone this affliction. Many even said that if they had a chance to do it differently, they would take on that same affliction.

As wonderful as the healing aspect of transformation is to behold, the thing that I have felt most strongly from people making these statements of gratitude is their sense of having accomplished their purpose, a purpose that was so important to them that they would not avoid that task if they were given the opportunity again.

MY KARMA

It is also important in the understanding of the laws of consciousness to test and examine the laws against one's own experience. My experience includes many very clear memories of prior life experiences in the earth. Memory of past-life experiences is not easily opened, and most people have no need to explore such memories. They see the laws at work in their own life and recognize that the work of transformation is today, not yesterday. It was helpful for me, prior to learning of the laws, to know from my own experience that, where appropriate, they operated beyond the limits of a single life experience.

The following experiences are taken from my own memory. They are memories I became aware of through my own efforts to recall what I assumed would be childhood experiences. I was supported in this process by a person who monitored my emotional responses, but did not in any way suggest to me subject matter or suggest that my recollections would be other than normal memories within this lifetime. There was no hypnosis, suggestion, or drugs of any type involved. Many of the memories I resisted and wanted to change because of their unpleasant nature, because of their strange physical effects on my body, and because I did not want to admit to myself that I performed many of the actions in these memories. My attempts to change them were not successful, because the force of the real events overrode the attempts I made to distort them. The few times I was consciously able to control a memory, it lost its sense of reality, and I recognized the invalidity of the alteration.

The memories began as I sought to remember earlier times in my life when I had experienced feelings of pain and loss. My memory took me to the death of a beloved grandfather. As those feelings were felt powerfully within, I asked myself to remember further back. There came to mind a clear memory of a different time and place. I was a young soldier holding a dying comrade who had been my friend. Although in a different place and time, it was I. In the memory of bearing loss, I also remembered being a young mother. My child and I were sick and starving. There was nothing and no one to help us. The child died first, and I promised her that sometime I would be able to give her love and care and the things her heart desired. My death followed shortly.

Day after day, week after week, as I searched out these emotions within me and followed them back to earlier experiences, my memories opened up. I remembered death after death. I died as a slave, beaten and mistreated. I died of disease and famine. As a woman, I remembered rape, slavery, and both the separation from and death of my family. As a man, I was often a soldier. My memories of these experiences were of death before one army after another, stabbed by swords, shot with arrows, and trampled under the feet of horses. As a child, I died of neglect, of famine, and by being abandoned to be torn apart by wild animals.

As I looked at these experiences, I finally reached the point of asking, "Why?" The question was answered with another memory. From our dress and activities, I estimate it was around the time of the conquests of Genghis Khan. I was a war leader and very effective. As a being who spread human misery, I was also very effective. It was so difficult for me to accept this memory. It stood before my eyes a long time before I could let myself acknowledge it. I never did have the courage to look at many parts. I remembered enough of my actions to understand that no army, no soldier, no famine, no person, and no condition I have ever experienced on the earth had brought to me any suffering that I had not first inflicted upon humankind. From my memories of suffering, I came to realize that the law works perfectly.

In some life in that process of learning I began to seek a different way of living. It was in living by giving instead of taking that my life experiences began to change. The only person I ever had to forgive for the lifetimes of suffering which my memories revealed to me was myself. Forgiveness heals and empowers the one who forgives.

Out of love and care for yourself, send your love and compassion to your hurt, then forgive. It is the door to your freedom.

Chapter 8

The Law of Wisdom

How much better to get wisdom than gold,
to choose understanding rather than silver!
Proverbs 16:16 (NIV)

There are a number of Universal Laws that result in our finding that which we are seeking, whether at the spiritual, mental, or physical levels of our experience. There are also laws that operate to bring us wisdom, guidance, answers, and solutions in our lives. It is this aspect of the law—guidance and wisdom—that I would like to share with you. If you will seek the guidance, then you can bring about harmoniously other goals you may hold for your life. If you do not work with the guidance, a good possibility exists that even if you fulfill your goals, you may not fulfill your heart.

The Law of Wisdom—"As you sincerely ask within yourself for guidance, it will be given."

ASKING FOR GUIDANCE IN TIMES OF GREAT CHANGE

More than thirty years ago, I began to study and apply the Edgar Cayce readings on guidance. During these years, I have worked with many aspects and processes of guidance and taught them to many people. Instructions received from applying that knowledge have guided the major decisions of my life, from marriage to jobs and many decisions of daily living. I came to know from personal experience that guidance is there for every situation.

By "guidance" I mean receiving wisdom from your higher self. It does not refer to psychic information or guides. The Cayce readings assure us that we all have this wisdom within us.

Several years ago, I found myself in a strange situation. Consulting my guidance led me to the understanding that we were moving into a time of extensive change, changes also foreshadowed by the readings. The effects of accelerating change were obvious in my own life and in the lives of the people with whom I worked. I realized that this time of change was deeply impacting all people.

What could I give to those studying with me that would help them move as harmoniously as possible through this time of change? The deeper I sought understanding, the more complex the picture became. The old rules did not work anymore, the things one did to relate to family, society, work, health, knowledge, and our spiritual and religious structures were changing so fast that we were losing our ability to relate effectively to these things. People needed another level of assistance to meet these challenging times. Only the wisdom from their higher selves could guide them through such changes.

Many of the forms of guidance I had used were the result of the lifestyle changes suggested by my study of spirituality and the Cayce readings. I lived a life of service and took extensive time for prayer, reflection, and meditation. I became a vegetarian and sought subtle balances of energy within myself and my world. Even though I am a rather shy and retiring person, I had grown in my love for people and enjoyed supporting them in living life more fully. These had all contributed to my ability to receive and understand my guidance. Even with my years of experience and spiritual practice, I still often had questions about my guidance. Was that really the guidance of my higher self, or was it my ego—my intellect—figuring out what I wanted to hear again?

Most of the people I was working with were open to spiritual growth, yet caught in very busy lives heavily impacted by rapid change. Taking the path of development that I had pursued in learning about my guidance was not a real option for them. It certainly was not for the many millions of people who were not even aware of these spiritual teachings and laws but were working hard and doing their best just to survive. They needed help now. For these people and for myself, as life accelerated, there had to be another answer. I decided to apply the Law of Wisdom. Sincerely, within myself, I invoked the Law of Wisdom by asking through prayer to be shown that answer.

Within a month, I found myself on an assignment that I thought was about spiritual education for children. I was meeting people who were a part of a nonprofit business called the Institute of HeartMath. I realized something in this situation was different than I had expected. Their effectiveness in their work and communication and their presence in listening and conversation was something I had wished for in many groups I had dealt with. I asked them about their work and began to learn about their insight into the heart, which they seemed to understand more completely than anyone I had heard before. They explained about the heart's relationship to guidance. I tested their ideas and techniques extensively. The results were superb.

Finally I had discovered the answer to my question. I had been led to the answer to my prayer. I now could offer the people with whom I worked a simple, easy way to receive guidance that was so effective that anyone, regardless of spiritual background or education, could get clear answers from his or her own higher self. This way put each directly in touch with the answers needed in the moment of experience without the need for interpretation. When the answer came, it also changed the perception and understanding of the situation so that the response from the heart became part of the solution.

The technique I learned was Freeze-Frame, which I explained in detail in chapter 5, "How to Love." It works so effectively because it works directly with the heart. The higher intelligence of the Divine enters your system through your heart where it is stepped down to the energy levels that can be utilized and processed through your body and brain. This is accomplished through the electromagnetic energy field that is generated by your heart. Accessing that field by specific techniques puts you in direct contact with that intelligence that can guide you in every aspect of life in which you desire assistance.

The first three steps of Freeze-Frame make the connection with the heart. The specific steps of Freeze-Frame that invoke the Law of Wisdom are the fourth and fifth steps in which you sincerely ask your heart a question and then listen for that answer. Take a moment and write that answer down. The more you acknowledge that answer and draw from that intelligence, the deeper will be the response and your understanding.

Just as the energies of our time are speeding things up, they are also bringing in higher intelligence and higher efficiency in guiding humankind through these times of change. These new higher fourth- and fifth-dimensional energies support our deeper connection with the heart and its wisdom. They make effective use of the Law of Wisdom.

Isn't that what we have all been asking for? To know what our lives are about and how to be effective at living them? Haven't you wanted to know how to meet the changes in your life in a way that would take you and those around you into a greater sense of fulfillment? Techniques such as Freeze-Frame and others that utilize the energy of the heart and its intuitive field are to my perception what we have drawn to ourselves through our sincere asking for meaningful answers that assist us in living in clarity and peace.

The other techniques we will be exploring in this chapter are also of value. They are important ways to strengthen one's spiritual connection. In whatever way you seek to apply the Law of Wisdom, the deeper your connection with your sincere heart feelings, the more effective will be your response.

SPIRITUAL MATURITY

The process of spiritual maturation consists of connecting with your spirit at deeper and deeper levels. Although some of the early work of connecting with God's infinite wisdom begins with work in the mind, at some point the focus of that work shifts to the heart and its direct connection with Spirit. Charles Fillmore, a turn-of-the-century American mystic and cofounder of the Unity movement, acknowledged some very important elements of wisdom in describing the unfolding relationship with heart intelligence.

When we discover in ourselves a flow of thought that seems to have been evolved independent of the reasoning process . . . one should give attention to this unusual and usually faint whispering of Spirit in man. It is not of the intellect and it does not originate in the skull. It is the development, in man, of a greater capacity to know himself and to understand the purpose of creation. The Bible gives many examples of the awakening of the brain of the heart, in seers, in lawgivers, and in prophets. It is accredited as coming from the heart.[1]

Fillmore describes the change of focus within the individual from the head to the heart as a natural process of spiritual illumination.

> Here the natural order of spiritual illumination is illustrated. Man receives first an intellectual understanding of Truth which he transmits to the heart, where love is awakened. The Lord reveals to him that the faculty of love is the greatest of all the powers of man and that head knowledge must decrease as heart understanding increases.[2]

The actual change that takes place is not a decrease of head knowledge but rather a new role for head knowledge. It becomes a facilitator for the heart wisdom. The head's role shifts from being the commander in chief of the system to being an effective general under the heart's leadership. That is the function for which the intellect was designed — to interpret the heart's intelligence into linear form. The intellect is brought to fulfillment as wisdom is sought in the heart.

ASK AND SEEK

Jesus taught people how to work with the Law of Wisdom in three simple steps that help us understand how we can put it to effective use in our lives. He said:

> Ask and it will be given to you;
> seek and you will find;
> knock and the door will be opened to you."
> Matthew 7:7 (NIV)

You know it isn't a law that you will get something if you ask for it. We all learned early as children that asking for candy in the checkout line at the grocery store doesn't often get us what we desire. You have probably also asked for, or perhaps paid for, advice that you later recognized was about the person's own life rather than yours, whether it was a lawyer, doctor, or friend giving the advice.

Sometimes it may seem foolish to ask within ourselves for guidance. After all, our best thinking is often what got us into our problems. The Cayce readings point out that the answer to every problem is to find the truth about the problem. The only viewpoint from which we can see the truth about the problem and learn the lesson it's bringing is to get to a consciousness higher than the one which created the problem. Since we inevitably create our problems by using our mental faculties, we need to go higher—to seek the spiritual level in our hearts where the truth is known. This is what happens when we sincerely ask within ourselves for guidance.

In fact, my experience of this law is that we get much more than guidance. We get answers and solutions. As I addressed the concern I had for helping others find a simple way of guidance, I not only received guidance that helped me recognize the answer when it was presented, I discovered a connection within where the answer was given. As you will see in the following examples, the response of life is to not only give guidance, but also to lead us to resolution, understanding, and discovery. Beyond the answers of words, we get the opportunity to embrace and live the answers.

CONNECTING WITH THE SOURCE

There are a number of effective ways of learning to attune to your spiritual self—to connect with your source of wisdom. You will discover that as you enter into a relationship and dialogue with your spiritual nature, you become increasingly receptive to your guidance.

In seeking this connection with the spiritual self, how we seek is important. The source of universal knowledge that Cayce tapped into offered this insight:

. . . if you seek for the gratifying of your own self alone, or how you may take advantage of your brother, then know the spirit of truth departs from you. Through whatever channel you may seek, *be sincere with yourself.* If you would have that which is the manifestation of the Spirit of the Father through any channel, be sincere with yourself; for like begets like. *The spirit of truth is nigh unto you . . . seek him in your own heart;* for your soul is the image of your Father—and as you seek in truth, as you seek in sincerity, as you seek, so will it be opened unto you. TODAY—if you will hear His voice. 5752-5 (Author's italics)AR

Through the Law of Wisdom, guidance becomes available to us if we choose to seek or ask for it. However, just because it is available and can assist us in the day-to-day experiences of living, does not mean we have to take it.

MAC AND DAVID

My friend Mac and I were involved in the selection of a house at the same time. We were both students of the Universal Laws. We knew that our spiritual nature was an active part of every life experience and that there was a wisdom available to guide us through any situation. Consequently, we both asked for guidance in determining the proper price to pay in purchasing our respective houses.

The price of the house chosen by Mac was $89,000. Mac sat quietly, asked his spiritual self the right price to pay, cleared his mind, and waited for the answer. The answer he got was $50,000. Although this price seemed very low, he called the seller and offered that amount. The seller turned his offer down, but feeling that he was guided in the matter, Mac decided to wait. Several months later the seller called Mac back and asked if the $50,000 offer was still open. Mac said it was and bought the house as he had been guided. He found his new home very beneficial to the changes he was making in his life.

I also asked for guidance in the purchase of my house. The house I was looking at was listed for $79,000. As I sat quietly, open to guidance, I asked if this was the right house. In answer to my question, the picture of another house I had looked at earlier entered my mind with the words, "Be patient." I asked the question, "If I bought the house listed for $79,000, what would be a fair price to offer?" After clearing my mind, I received the number $68,000. My realtor told me the house was probably priced fairly and that $68,000 was an unreasonably low offer. I bought the house for $75,000.

The next year several changes occurred in my life, and I needed a larger house. I ended up buying the house first shown to me by my guidance, which served my family's needs well. After trying for some time to sell the original house, it sold for $68,000—the price my guidance had originally given. If I had listened to my guidance, I would have been a lot farther ahead than the $7,000 I lost on the purchase price.

The Laws of Attunement make guidance and wisdom available to us in all phases of life. They do not require that we follow the guidance.

WAYS OF RECEIVING GUIDANCE

There are many ways we can receive guidance. Not all of those are the result of the Law of Wisdom. During a seminar some years ago I asked the participants to write down the ways they receive guidance. I was amazed at the variety of methods used. There were over forty different methods of receiving guidance. They fell into three categories:

- The first was inner asking and response—listening to one's inner wisdom without an outer stimulus.
- The second was using an outer stimulus to trigger one's inner wisdom, such as the words of a song or opening the Bible and spotting a particular passage.
- The third was outer guidance—from friends to professionals to psychics.

The Law of Wisdom operates from one's own heart intelligence. A person can hear advice from others; however, one must always check it against one's own wisdom. Simply drawing a response from the outer is not a guarantee of its applicability to your life.

OUTER GUIDANCE

I've heard many people tell me, "Oh, I just saw this. It must be a sign I should do so and so." Well, maybe it was and maybe it wasn't. You don't know from the outer. Check the inner with your heart intelligence. Maybe it was just your way of finally justifying what you wanted to do anyway. If you don't connect with the guidance from your higher self, how would you know what was meant by the sign you saw or the advice you received? Fortunately, having seen the "sign," read the words, or heard the psychic, now you are in touch with how you feel so that you can check those feelings out in your heart intelligence.

STILL, SMALL VOICE

A major emphasis of the Cayce readings and a condition of the Law of Wisdom are that you should seek guidance within yourself. By proper attunement you can go directly to the source.

There is in all of us that still Voice that teaches sacrifice, love, and service, that warns of every catastrophe and protects from all danger. When it is listened to and followed, no mistakes are made, no wars are fought, no homes are broken up; for then we seek the good of our neighbors and the will of the Creator.[3]

That still voice is the intuitive connection with the intelligence or the wisdom within your own heart. Your heart is filled with that intelligence—the pattern or blueprint of your soul. The prophet Jeremiah acknowledged this relationship of the connection of God's higher wisdom and law with the heart.

I will put my law within them, and I will write it upon their hearts; and I will be their God, and they shall be my people. Jeremiah 31:33 (RSV)

Sara Paddison, who had developed her own ability to make an inner connection with that pattern through her application of these laws, sincerely asked to see and understand how it was possible for this pattern and intelligence to be found in the heart. She saw that at the core of the heart exists a personal blueprint, a pattern that was also holographically a part of our DNA. She has described the etheric structure that holds the pattern as "heart crystals." In her book, The Hidden Power of the Heart, she described her insight into this pattern:

. . . An image of seemingly infinite crystals appeared in a cornucopia shape. The cornucopia was filled with crystal-like formations. I saw many facets and edges. I realized that each crystal edge held a different intelligent frequency band. Each facet seemed to hold a different program or pattern.
To my amazement, I realized that each individual human being has his or her own particular heart crystal pattern and colors and I saw this as the soul's blueprint. There

were chips that contained detailed information: storage records of this life, past lives, and future possibilities—the whole intelligence of the human being.[4]

The heartfelt sincerity of our asking influences those crystals as does the intelligence entering our system through the intuitive field. That intelligence is able to bring fresh perspective and understanding in response to our asking. From this connection given through the still, small voice of the heart, we are unfolding the divine pattern within us—our own divine plan.

WAYS OF INNER CONNECTION

The readings and different spiritual and religious paths offer many approaches to seeking within. Here are five basic ways or methods of making this inner connection that are strongly emphasized by the readings:

1. Go within
2. Meditation
3. Study of dreams
4. Walk and talk with Him
5. Prayer

1. Go Within

Enter into better communication with Him within self. Be willing to say: Not my will but yours be done. Use me as you see fit; rather than I am willing—but let me tell you how! Listen—listen to that within and you will have your answer. (2174-3)AR

To go within is basically to turn your attention, your mind, your energy from the outer to the inner with a seeking spirit. How you do it is not as important as that you do it. You may do so in whatever way suits you best, whether it be one of those suggested above or any other form of contemplation, concentration, relaxation, reverie, or meditation. The act of dropping the outer, turning within, recognizing that the true power and wisdom is within you is the key, whether you do it for two minutes, ten minutes, or an hour. Turning within makes the difference and gets the results. Obviously the more you can do it in a balanced way, in the spirit of truly seeking, the better.

HELEN ELLINGTON

Helen Ellington was an older woman who lived near Mr. Cayce and became interested in his work. She was a member of his Bible class and was also a member of the first Search for God study group founded in Norfolk, Virginia. Here Amanda Wakester passes on a delightful tale Helen told of how she began to get guidance—a tale which illustrates very well how going within has very little to do with technique but how important your thoughts and attitudes about it are:

"I was in Bible Class, and Mr. Cayce said, 'If you can ask a question, you can answer it.' I'd heard him say that a time or two before, and I was too timid to ask what it meant."

"So, finally, I said, 'Excuse me, Mr. Cayce. If you can answer a question, why will you ask it?'

"And he looked at m.e . . . He was utterly surprised that I didn't know what he was talking about—but I didn't. He said, 'Don't ask somebody else; ask yourself. If you didn't have the answer, you couldn't formulate the question to start with.'

"I thought, well, now I'm just as puzzled as I was before. I still didn't understand what he meant. I said, 'I'll have to put it to the test.'

"I had been getting readings for the family and different ones and [would] always write out a list of questions to have them ready to get the information. Most every time I'd write a question after that, the answer would come right to me. And I caught myself doing that so often that I was reminded that Mr. Cayce might be right. But I said, 'I know I don't know everything. I've got to find a question I can't answer.'

"I went downtown to a lecture one night—the whole group went. The man was giving a good lecture, and I was enjoying every word of it, listening intently. All at once he said, 'The only way we can ever know God is to want to know Him more than anything else. And the only way we can really know Him is to experience Him.'

"I thought, oh, what a statement! And my mind went 'round like a spin button. I lost track of what the man was talking about, I didn't hear another word he said, I forgot everything he'd said before. I came home with my mind still going 'round and 'round. I thought, well, that's a question I know that I can't answer.

"'How can I experience God?' was my question, and I got no answer. I kept on asking it. I didn't tell anybody all this was going on; I just kept it to myself.

"This continued for several months. I began to think: 'I'll never get the answer to that one, I know I won't.' Then one day I went into the bathroom to pick up the laundry bag to give to the wetwash man, and I saw something somebody had dropped on the floor. As I stooped down to pick it up, a voice started passing through my mind—like somebody was talking to me. I didn't hear it, but it came into my consciousness just as if I were hearing it. And it made a statement, slowly, one word at a time. And I stopped right still. It said: 'If-you-would-experience-God-you-must-be-God-to-somebody-else.'

"I said, 'Oh me, that's my answer. I know that's the answer. That is the answer—for me, if for nobody else.' I thanked the Lord from the bottom of my heart for that.

At first it never occurred to her that she could use this technique for other than philosophical questions. A good while after that, she and her daughter Margaret were washing dishes and discussing some of the things that were coming through the readings.

"Every time I'd start to talk, I'd start to cough."

Helen had been bothered with this cough for a couple of years. She didn't have a cold or seem to have any lung trouble, but she felt a knot, a tightness, in the pit of her stomach that caused her cough.

"I was so tired of coughing. I'd almost coughed myself to death. I said, 'Well, Margaret, if there's any truth in what Mr. Cayce says, I think it's time I asked myself what's causing me to have this cough.' And I took a plate and set it down with a vengeance on the dining room table.

"As I set the plate down, that same voice came back: 'Don't you remember that day you were putting preserves up on the shelf?'

Helen remembered a Sunday morning two years earlier. She had done some canning the day before and had left the jars in the kitchen to cool. Rushing to get ready for church, she grabbed a chair for a footstool and began putting the jars away in the pantry, going back and forth with a jar in each hand and having to step a bit too high to reach the chair each time. In doing so, she twisted her back and thought, then, that she'd have to see the osteopath. By night, the pain was so severe that she couldn't lie on her back. She'd had a lot of adjustments and had some idea of how they were done. With a little self-treatment, she finally relieved the pain enough so that she could lie down.

The voice continued: "You thought you had a kink in your back, and you thought you got it out. Well, you didn't get it all out. You need to have that straightened out, and then your cough will leave."

Margaret took her for an adjustment the next day. The adjustment was a success. She gives Edgar Cayce the credit.

"By knowing to ask myself that question and waiting for an answer, I got the problem corrected. I have done that two or three times since then. That's the reason I've been able to live as long as I have."

Although a member of the first Study Group, Helen was never comfortable with formal, group meditation. Her self-questioning technique, this deep pondering, became, in a sense, her method of meditation.

"I don't sleep, sometimes, too much at night. I just lie in bed and reason out things. Then sometimes I don't even have the words to describe what I learn."[5]

2. Meditation

Bruce describes his relationship to meditation the following way:

For me meditation has been one of the surest, most effective methods of attunement. When I first started to meditate I began doing it for fifteen minutes a day. I hoped it would work, but could not possibly imagine how it could make much difference; yet I was willing to give it a try. In the beginning, I had no great experiences, no lights flashed or visions or anything. My thoughts kept intruding, but I used a simple affirmation such as "peace" or "be still and know" to get rid of them. I was not even sure I was meditating, but I had to admit that things at work seemed to go smoother. However I did not feel I could give the credit to meditation for I could not see any change in myself. But when my teenage son asked: "What happened, you're different?" and my wife nodded vigorously in agreement, I knew I was on to something.

Basically meditation is another way in which we can turn self around, to make the shift of our attention from the outer to the inner and to recognize there is something there we need. It is a means by which we can train our minds to allow us to become aware of the Divine within. You have to learn to meditate. However, it comes easily for most, and much excellent help and material are available.

Cayce's source explained to one young man that if he would find his purpose, set and live his ideals in accord with that purpose, and meditate consistently, he would become aware of his attunement with the Spirit within. This awareness would bring to him the ability to meet whatever issues faced him, and he could become a might and a power in meeting the needs of the hour. [6]

To another individual the readings made a startling statement: That the wisdom of God surpassed the understanding of man *except* for that gained in his meditations.[7]

As to getting guidance through meditation, there are no limits, as this classic interchange emphasized:

Q. Is it possible to meditate and obtain needed information?

A. On any subject! Whether you are going digging for fishing worms or playing a concerto! (1861-12)

So meditation is of great assistance to your attunement, to your seeking, to your guidance, and to your decision making. Bruce says:

I began those first meditations more than twenty-five years ago and feel without any doubt my daily meditations have been by far the most rewarding and valuable aspects of my life, for they have really totally changed me and my life for the better and given it a consistency and quality beyond anything I could possibly have imagined when I started. The greatest gift or favor you can bestow on yourself and others with whom you associate is to meditate daily.

From experimenting with many techniques over the years, I have come to appreciate the addition of the focus on the heart in my meditation. That and the resting in inner silence have been the elements that have brought to me personally the deepest consistent experiences of quality and regeneration.

3. Study of Dreams

Remember, dreams are but a pattern of that whole. For what is the premise? Your Lord is One.

Then as the physical consciousness is laid aside, there may come dreams or visions, and even He, your Lord, your Brother, may show you. For He is the same yesterday, today and forever. And He has promised to speak with you, if you desire same; possibly in dreams, in visions, or in the still small voice within.

Trust not other means! (1992-1)AR

JOB CHOICES

At one point in my life I faced a major employment decision, and I sincerely asked within for guidance as to what was for my highest good. I set a three-day period to receive my guidance. During that time I received a series of three dreams. In them I saw the three jobs being offered me, each in law, my career field. In the first dream, I walked into my former office, and a woman who worked there came in and set before me a scale model of a volcano that was ready to explode. In the second dream, I saw a large but empty house which I knew to be mine in the town of my second job opportunity. I was impressed with its size, emptiness, and loneliness. In the third dream, I saw the law library in the building where I would be working if I took the third offer. It was old, dusty, and boring, but as I looked up, I saw a window at the end of a row of books through which the sun was shining.

The dreams did not tell me which way to go. I was free to make any choice I wanted. Looking at the first dream, I understood that to return to my old position would be to enter a situation which, like the volcano, would be explosive and possibly destructive. This turned out to be an accurate description of situations that eventually unfolded in that office. The second dream showed me only a large house, a symbol of what I could accomplish in the outer. Meaning and satisfaction were not there, only emptiness, which symbolized to me the lack of personal fulfillment I would find. The third dream showed a boring, mundane experience. However, the sunlit window at the end held a vision of meaning, possibility, and light which promised personal satisfaction.

From the dreams I chose the last job. As the dream foretold, much of it was routine, research-oriented work which I did not particularly enjoy. After several months some cases came to my attention that moved me into a new and personally satisfying area of work with consumer law. In this new area I was also able to see many of the laws of consciousness demonstrated which helped me develop the understandings that eventually led to my change of careers.

FREEZE-FRAME IT

Certainly dreams have helped me receive my guidance. But the truth is, at this point in my life, if I were facing those same questions again, I would do a Freeze-Frame on each question. In the deep, sincere contact with my heart through the Freeze-Frame experience, I would expect to have that wisdom put before me clearly and concisely. This doesn't mean you won't benefit from studying your dreams. Your dreams are a part of you, and it is helpful to be in touch with your whole self. However, in retrospect as I look now at those dreams, I would have liked to have had a Freeze-Frame to check out whether or not I was correctly interpreting my dreams.

4. Walk and Talk with Him

What do you feel is in the way of preventing Him from walking and talking with you? The readings advise that you put that question out of your mind. It is not a factor. He will walk and talk with you regardless. For myself it took me a long time to come to believe that I could talk with the Spirit within, that it would work for me, that I was good enough. Fortunately none of those things matter. You don't have to do a thing but try it.

"HIM"

I have a close friend who joined with me in prayer at the time

I asked for a way to help those I was working with find an efficient way of guidance. She was a cominister with me in the church at that time. She was also asking for her next level of understanding to fulfill her life purpose. A month later I found myself at the Institute of HeartMath in California, and she found herself at Satya Sai Baba's ashram in India. She has continued her studies with this wonderful being who is bringing great love and wisdom to our world.

Recently we met in the town where we had ministered together. She shared with me some of her experiences, and the essence of her sharing was that she walks and talks with Sai Baba. Through her heart she is receptive to his guidance for her, and he supports her in hearing her own inner wisdom at the very highest level.

The "Him" that Cayce speaks of will be "God" for some people; for others Jesus; for others Sai Baba, Mother Mary, or another great spiritual presence; and for others it will be their own higher wisdom and intelligence which they connect with when they are focused sincerely in their hearts.

AN EXAMPLE

Both of your authors have experienced a wonderful example of this teaching in their lives. We have seen the Law of Wisdom proven again and again through the presence of this person who is wife to one of us and mother to the other. The wisdom she has brought has guided our lives and her talks with the Presence have greatly enriched our family. For her, the activities of life — whether preparing a meal, doing research, or caring for a grandchild — are filled with her contact with the Divine.

The decisions of her life have left the clear understanding that you do not know what you might be guided to do until you ask. Once you ask, the very best in your life will follow, if you will act on what you have been given. It is her example that has endeared the following reading to my heart, for in her example I have seen both the humbleness and the glory.

> . . . this is the attitude for an entity to take. *Walk* with Him! *Talk* with Him! See *Him* as He manifests in every form of life; for He *is* life in *all* its manifestations in the earth! and there will come that peace, that harmony, that understanding, that comes from *humbleness* in *His* name; humbleness

of spirit, of mind, of self, that the glories that are your own *from* the foundations of the earth may be manifested *in* you! (488-6)AR

Take a walk—take Him along—ask Him to come with you as you would a friend. Talk with Him about the weather, the flowers, the traffic, the groceries. If you forget what you came for, ask Him. He will remind you. Really, really talk with Him. Verbally or in thought, speak openly. Nothing is off limits. Nothing is unimportant to Him if it concerns you or is of interest to you.

I have found this process of walking and talking with Him to be very worthwhile and practical. I'm more absentminded than I care to admit and always end up somewhere not having what I intended to bring, leaving what I was supposed to take. I have learned that if I ask Him before I leave, "Do I have everything I'm supposed to?" If the answer is no or if there is no answer, then I start looking for what's missing. If the answer is yes, I can go without concern. Of course, being absentminded, I forget to ask sometimes! I'm working on that, too!

Likewise, if someone asks me to do something, I can ask Spirit, "Should I?" and get the answer right then if necessary. The process saves me both time and money for it automatically shapes up my life and keeps me in balance—when I use it. When I fail to use it, I find myself wasting time, overcaring, and getting into things not in line with my purpose.

In using this process for finding the answers, you need to give it a sincere try. Some people at first hear nothing. If that happens, don't conclude it isn't working for you. Like anything of value, it takes some practice mainly because maybe for years you may have believed you couldn't do it, or that it was crazy, or that God was up there on a cloud and would not assist you in your life. To change that kind of consciousness may take some effort. Forget all that intellectual garbage, for you are now dealing with spiritual law. Open yourself to walking and talking with Him. The law is: "As you sincerely ask within yourself for guidance, it will be given."

5. Prayer

The fifth way of inner connection is through the experience of prayer. This can be a meaningful and profound experience, and it can also be a meaningless exercise. The difference is—where is your attention? Is it in your head or your heart? If prayer is a sincere connecting with Spirit for you, enjoy it and bring your questions to it.

Emerson set an ideal for prayer when he gave this inspired definition: "Prayer is the contemplation of the facts of life from the highest point of view." Mother Teresa of Calcutta in her book, *The Love of Christ*, speaks inspiringly of prayer:

> Love prayer. Feel often the need to pray, and take the trouble to pray. It is by praying often that you will pray better. Prayer enlarges the heart until it is capable of containing the gift that God makes of Himself. Ask and seek; your heart will grow capable of receiving Him and holding on to Him. [8]

The Cayce readings contained a great deal about prayer. At one point Cayce recommended formation of a prayer group for those interested in his work—to pray for anyone who requested it. That prayer group continues today. If you would like their prayer support, send your requests to: Glad Helpers Healing Prayer Group, Association for Research and Enlightenment, P. O. Box 595, Virginia Beach, VA 23451-0595.

Of great help on a daily basis is a little booklet called *Daily Word*, which is put out monthly for a very modest fee. It has a prayer for each day, which is very much in accord with the philosophy expressed in the Cayce readings. This publication is nondenominational and has a circulation of more than two million copies monthly! The organization that publishes that booklet, Silent Unity, is unique. It has prayed for others at their request since 1890. For nearly one hundred years—a remarkable record—prayer has been held continuously twenty-four hours a day. The number of prayer requests this organization receives, more than three million last year, attests to the effectiveness of their help. Anyone can call—there are no charges. Telephone prayer requests are taken around the clock, and a call made to them is a spiritual experience in itself. The telephone number is 816-251-2100. If you prefer to write, the address is: Silent Unity, Unity Village, MO 64065.

Many times we just sense a need or are dealing with a confusing condition and don't really know what to ask for. Fortunately if we appeal for help, Spirit will give us what we need. The point is to ask. There is an old prayer of the Kond tribe in Tibet that fits all cases:

O God, I do not know what is best
for me, but You do and for that I pray.

Another way to respond when we do not know how to address
the situations before us is to utilize the question suggested in
the Freeze-Frame exercise. Remember, this exercise is designed
to take anyone, whether clear or confused, to the place of intuitive heart response. The question is:

"What is the most efficient response to this situation, one
that will minimize future stress?"

Why pray with a question like efficiency and minimizing
stress? Because there is such love for you and such wisdom
available that it would have you move as effortlessly as possible,
as harmoniously as possible, through the issues that you are
facing in your life. That is the great care of the divine intelligence
for you.

KNOCK AND THE DOOR WILL BE OPENED TO YOU

One of the most important elements of our receiving guidance
is the part of asking. We have looked at asking and seeking as
Jesus encouraged us in working with the Law of Wisdom. The
third part of His instruction was, "Knock and the door will be
opened to you."

Then may you as seekers of the way, may you that have
come seeking to know, to experience, to *feel* that presence
of the Christ Consciousness within your own breast, within
your own experience, *open* the door of your heart!
For He stands ready to enter, to those who will bid Him
enter.
He comes not unbidden, but as you seek you find; as you
knock it is opened. As you live the life is the awareness of
His closeness, of His presence, yours. (5749-10)AR

When you knock, you are recognizing that you have come as far
as you can on your own. Only the higher power that exists within
you can open the door that stands before you safely and completely. You accept this reality and put your trust in that divine
presence within you by knocking. As you do, the door will open.

KNOCKING FOR KNOWLEDGE

I was drawn to knock on the door of knowledge and challenge the teaching that all knowledge is within. I asked to know if I really did have access to all wisdom. At the time I was entering a new field of study and work in which I had very little knowledge. As a result of my asking, I became unable to read the many fine books in my field. I could not read any of them. When I would open one, someone would call, or if there were no distractions, I would fall asleep. I even tried to get around this blockage by scheduling classes to teach the books. I still could not read the book before the class; however, in the class I could read a line, and I would understand it in the context of the entire book. I could only get through a line or two each class.

I had to rely on my own guidance and inner wisdom throughout my studies and well into my career. During that time I wanted very much to use the academic tools that had always been a major part of my life; however, with my access to outer forms of knowledge cut off, I had to depend on whatever came through that inner door upon which I had knocked. Eventually I was able to pick up and read the book that eight years earlier had prompted my question. However, this time when I found the assertion that all knowledge was within, I knew the door of knowledge was now open.

KNOCKING FOR UNDERSTANDING

Perhaps the greatest challenge for me with the experience of knocking was in seeking to understand the murder of my wife just weeks before the first birthday of our child. I could not perceive that God was absolute and all good when such a thing could happen. From that knocking, I can assure you that everything you seek can be found. My questions were many, and there were many trips to that door before all my questions were answered. But all of them were answered. Even when that seeking brought me knowledge and information from outside sources, it was only by sincerely knocking on the door of understanding within myself that I could evaluate the validity of that information.

The difficulty for those who would use this law is not that the door will not open, nor that anything, including the very deepest parts of oneself, is hidden behind a door that will remain closed. All doors will open, and there is nothing in the universe that is secret from those willing to sincerely seek it. The difficulty is that of being able to accept what is found there and to live in accord with what it means. Because of that I must warn you that when you use this law, you are attempting one of the most demanding uses of the laws; yet its gifts are great.

UNANTICIPATED RESPONSES

I hope that you are beginning to see that there are many ways in which guidance responds to us when we ask. I have mentioned several times the importance of the heart connection. I do not mean to say that inner contact and guidance is not possible without the heart connection, only that it is more difficult. My experience has been that the deeper the heart connection, the more direct the guidance can be.

CHARLES FILLMORE

Charles Fillmore, learned to establish this contact with Spirit without the heart connection. As Myrtle Fillmore's husband, he was deeply affected by his wife's healing. Prior to the awakening that took him into the role of spiritual leadership, he decided, "If I am Spirit and this God they talk so much about is Spirit, we can somehow communicate, or the whole thing is a fraud." So Charles, being a practical businessman, began an experiment:

I then commenced sitting in the silence every night at a certain hour and tried to get in touch with God. There was no enthusiasm about it; no soul desire, but a cold calculating business method. I was there on time every night and tried in all conceivable ways to realize that my mind was in touch with the Supreme Mind.

In this cold, intellectual attitude one can easily understand why I did not seem to get any conscious results, but I kept at it month after month, mentally affirming words that others told me would open the way, until it got to be a habit and I rather enjoyed it.

However, a time came when I began to observe that I was having exceedingly realistic dreams. For months I paid no attention to them, my business at that time being of the earth, earthly—buying and selling real estate. The first connection that I observed between the dreams and my affairs was after closing the purchase of a piece of property, I remembered that I had dreamed about the whole transaction some months before.

After that I watched my dreams closely and found that there was a wider intelligence manifesting in my sleep than I seemed to possess in the waking state, and it flashed over me one day that this was the mode of communication that had been established in response to my desire for information from headquarters. This has been kept up ever since with growing interest on my part, and I could fill a large book with my experiences. Everything which it is necessary for me to know is shown to me, and I have times without number been saved from false steps by this monitor. Again and again, I have had mapped out the future along certain lines for months and years ahead, and the prophecies have so far never failed, although I have sometimes misinterpreted the symbols used.[10]

CHECKING YOUR GUIDANCE

How do you know that the guidance you are receiving is from your higher self? I check the quality of feeling I am experiencing when receiving that guidance. When I feel peace, assurance, and a sense of knowing or understanding, the guidance has proven to be wise, practical, and effective.

Guidance from Spirit never will suggest that you take advantage of someone or require that you harm or deprive yourself or another of anything really needed in any way. If you get such guidance, it is not from Spirit but from other sources.

You can check your guidance to make sure it is from Spirit within you by the standards given to a young woman who was a counselor. She wanted to know how she could be sure her guidance was truly from Spirit within and not her imagination, emotions, desires, or other sources. Cayce's source gave these practical suggestions for checking the source of her guidance:

> [Does it speak] of kindness, gentleness, patience—that threshold upon which godliness appears? . . .
> Does it bring, then, self-abstinence? or does it bring self-desire?
> Does it bring love? Does it bring self-control? Is it gentle? Is it kind?

Then, these be the judgments upon which the entity uses those influences upon the lives of others.

Does it relieve suffering, as the abilities of the entity grow?

Does it relieve the mental anguish, the mental disturbances which arise?

Does it bring also healing—of body, of mind, to the individual? Is it healed for constructive force, or for that as will bring pain, sorrow, hate, and fear into the experience of others?

These be the judgments upon which the entity makes its choices, as it guides, directs or gives counsel to those who are seeking—seeking—What? That Light—which has become, which is, which ever has been the light of the world! (1947-3)AR

Chapter 9

The Master Law of Relationships

Before receiving
There must be giving.

He who does not trust enough
will not be trusted.

They do not quarrel,
so no one quarrels with them.

The sage never tries to store things up.
The more he does for others, the more he has.
The more he gives to others, the greater his abundance.

Lao Tsu

The Master Law of Relationships—"As you do to others, so will it be done to you."

Judge not, and you will not be judged; condemn not, and you will not be condemned; forgive, and you will be forgiven; give, and it will be given to you; good measure, pressed down, shaken together, running over, will be put into your lap. For the measure you give will be the measure you get back.

Jesus   (Luke 6:37-38 RSV)

One of the fundamental rules of life that has come to us through the ages is: "Do unto others as you would that others should do unto you." You and I know this as the Golden Rule. The great significance of this ancient teaching is beautifully expressed in this excerpt from a reading:

> It is simple in words, yet so deep in its meaning, so far-reaching in its application in every phase of human experience! For it is the opposite of greed, avarice, hate, and that which makes people afraid. (2170-1)

Indeed that is so because in practicing this teaching we will naturally treat others with love as that is the way we all wish to be treated. Love is the opposite of greed, avarice, hate, and that which makes people afraid. The Master Law of Relationships is one of the Laws of Cause and Effect. However, when we do respond with love, we bring to this law the transforming power of the Law of Love. It is there that we find the true fulfillment available to us in our relationships.

Jesus in His Sermon on the Mount emphasized it in this way: "Therefore, all things whatsoever ye would that men should do to you, do you even so to them; for this is the law and the prophets." (Matthew 7:12 AV) I think it was His way of saying this is how you must live to be in accord with God's laws, as the prophets have been teaching for hundreds of years.

LAW OR TEACHING?

We know that a true Universal Law cannot be broken. The readings refer to "Do unto others as you would that they should do unto you" as a law. However, the statement in that form is not a law for it can be broken by doing unto others things you certainly would not want them to do to you. Both Jesus and Cayce's source were teaching how to use the law, rather than giving a direct statement of it. What is the basic unbreakable Universal Law they were teaching? It is the Master Law of Relationships, one of the Laws of Transformation which we can call the Golden Law.

The Golden Law—"As you do to others, it will be done to you."

The Golden Law is at one level one of the Laws of Cause and Effect. What you do to others is the cause by which you set the law in operation. What is done to you is the effect you have created. On the other hand, the Golden Rule is really a statement from a high consciousness viewpoint of how you can readily apply this law in your life. The following reading makes a wonderful suggestion of how to do this:

> Just be kind, just be gentle, just make for those expressions of these in your dealings with others. And these bring contentment and peace and happiness through the law: As you do unto others, so will it be done unto you; for you are applying the teaching: As you would that others should do to you, then do you even so to them. (805-4)P

UNIVERSALITY OF THE LAW

Eric Butterworth, well-known author and lecturer, also emphasizes for us the great importance of this law. He says:

> This is the principle of action and reaction—give and receive—the law of complementarity. Do as you would be done by, think as you would like to experience, love and you shall be love . . . forgive and you shall be forgiven. Jesus did not announce this as a new law. He did not create laws; He simply discovered them as part of the Divinity of Man. It is a principle as old as time, as inexorable as gravity, as impersonal as sunlight.
>
> When we think good, speak good, do good, we not only tend to pay debts of past limitations, we prepare the way for inevitable future blessings. Call it karma, call it cause and effect, call it the law of compensation—for it is a fundamental truth of life, and a most needed realization for all who would live life effectively.[1]

As Butterworth points out, a Universal Law is a part of the human dynamic. Here is its expression in some of the world's major religions:

> Judaism: "What is hateful to you, do not to your fellow man; that is the entire law; all the rest is commentary." (Hillel)

Buddhism: "All men shrink from suffering and all love life; remember that you too are like them; make your own self the measure of others, and so abstain from causing hurt to them" (Dhammapada)

Mohammed: "Do to all men as you would wish to have done unto you; and reject for others what you would reject for yourselves." (Hadith)

From the Hindu Vedas: "Do not to others what you do not wish done to yourself; and wish for others too what you desire and long for, for yourself–this is the whole of Dharma, heed it well." (Mahabharata)

Confucius: "Do not unto others what you would not have them do unto you."[2] (Analects)

Because we are dealing with a Universal Law, the results flow as a matter of law. Cayce stressed their inevitable result.

Also know that what you sow, in mental, material, and physical relationships, will be measured back to you again.

Then, have that policy to do unto others as you would have others do to you. *Expect* that! *Live* that in your dealings!

And you will find that He who is the Giver of all good and perfect gifts will bring to your experiences not only harmony and peace but greater opportunities, with material, social, and financial success. (1634-1)AR

APPLYING THE GOLDEN RULE

When Bruce first began working with this law many years ago, he had a real opportunity to put it to work.

I was threatened with a lawsuit. I had purchased some land and was suddenly faced with a lawsuit filed by the seller demanding payment far greater than I had anticipated from the contract. I felt that both my understanding of the contract and legal precedent were in my favor, and my attorney assured me that I could win the case.

The Golden Rule, however, says "do unto others as you would have them do to you." In trying to apply this to my situation I imagined myself in the other man's position. I decided that if I were he, I would like to be listened to and given consideration even if I was not completely correct. So rather than going ahead with the lawsuit, I arranged to have my attorney work out a reasonable compromise.

It was a good feeling to have a Universal Law to apply to the situation rather than to rely solely on attorneys, courts, judges, and manmade laws. Anyone who has had experience with even the best of such knows how uncertain the results may be. Why? It is not that attorneys, courts, and judges are not doing their best to be fair, but the result in the end will depend not upon the manmade laws, but on how you have used the Universal Laws.

If I had gone ahead and fought the case, even though I felt I was sure to win, I could well have lost, for the universe doesn't care about such things. It would have given me a lesson in "as you do unto others, so it will be done unto you." Since I applied the Universal Law in the best way I knew, I did not need that lesson and was able to settle the case on a friendly and peaceable basis, one with which we could both live.

Note the great wisdom in both this law and the Golden Rule. It does not require any standards of you other than your own— you decide how you would like to be treated if you were in the other person's place, then apply that to the other person. The Golden Rule gives no pat answer to how you must treat anyone. I may do it one way, you may do it another under similar circumstances, and we can both be right. The only requirement and the key, if you wish to change your relationships with others, is to treat others as you would wish to be treated.

BUSINESS AND COMMUNITIES

In spite of our ability to comprehend that a law is universal and works at all times, in all places for everyone, there are some areas we seem to exclude from the higher laws. Business has become one of these, seeming to have its own standards that give little consideration to the other person. According to Cayce, not only does the Master Law of Relationships apply to business relationships, it applies to groups, even cities. This question was asked of the sleeping Cayce:

Q. Is there any specific direction or activity in my present business that would lead to greater productivity and outlet for my talents and abilities?

A. As you would that others should do to you, do you so to them. This is not merely a tale or an axiom, but this *in* action creates greater actions that offer opportunities in business, in social, in the economic forces, in home relations and those of every nature. (1603-1)AR

It would be misleading to imply that because a person started acting consciously on this law that everything would suddenly change. This law is not an aspirin to take away the symptom like a headache. Rather it brings a fundamental healing and realignment of those things that are out of balance in a relationship— whether that is a business or family relationship. It works best when utilized with patience.

To an executive who had been trying to help others and had been condemned both by those he had helped and by others, the wisdom that came through was:

Be *patient* and you shall see the glory of the Father manifested in the lives, not only of those that have condemned or do condemn you for singleness of purpose, but in doing that which makes for oneness in your relationships to your fellow man, you shall *see* that they—your efforts—shall not, will not, go unrewarded in *any* direction. Be patient. (802-2)AR

The Universal Laws apply not only to each one of us as individuals, but also to our groups, businesses, associations, government, and even nations. During the Depression years, a businessman asked Cayce's source, while Cayce was in his trance state, if there was a message for his associates and the world. Indeed there was, and Cayce told him that it was not enough to seek for personal gain or even personal growth, but that all must come to realize that they have a spiritual relation to others which is: "I am my brother's keeper." He was told further that until the world and those in authority and those with power, financially, socially, commercially, or spiritually, recognized that each group and each individual is dependent upon one another, little progress of a lasting nature could be made. [3]

Then the source in a fascinating statement pointed to an example of a city which was different, one which had recognized these principles and applied them and so prosperity had come to it in spite of conditions elsewhere.

What cities are in the greater position of returned prosperity for their people? Cincinnati? Why? For it in many channels long ago adopted what? The Golden Rule, as that manner in which many of those in authority in the various groups would deal not only with their employees but with those whom they served. . .and these are the bases or the backgrounds, for you are your brother's keeper. (257-134)AR

A HIGHER LAW

This Universal Law works when applied. However, the law works at several different levels. We can easily see the cause-and-effect aspects of this law. From our own living we know that what we do returns to us. However, there is a higher aspect of this law. We can connect with our heart's wisdom for ourselves and others. That heart's desire is for the experience of love, peace, and harmony. This law becomes the instrument for bringing that into our lives. As we express to others the care, love, and understanding that we desire in our lives, we are unleashing the transformative power of the Law of Love. Cayce described it this way:

[It] is not man's problem alone to be good, but to be good *for something,* to be good as a purposefulness!
   . . . you have *known* and you do know in your heart of hearts the ways of good! Not that of long-facedness, not that of the saintly sinner, not that of the cynic; but doing good for Good's sake, doing good because it brings contentment, it brings harmony, it brings peace, it brings associations that create in the hearts of the associates *joy* and *hope* and the *longing* for the greater knowledge of the *source* of good. Not just good but *being,* acting, thinking in terms of that honest, due consideration for each and every individual, and not the advantage by chance, not the advantage by foreknowledge, not the advantage in any way or manner over your fellow man.
   For as in the manner you treat your fellow man you treat your Maker. (417-8)AR

Edgar Cayce's source called the Golden Law the Universal Blessing and indeed it is, both for those to whom you apply it and for yourself when you apply it to others. He put great emphasis on this law as the instrument through which you can create many of the qualities you desire to find in your relationships. Beyond simply receiving back what you are giving out, he speaks of the law as providing a spiritual connection and a transformative result.

> The gospel of the Christ is, to do unto others as you would have others do unto you — and do it *every* day, in *every* way. And thus may His power, His glory, be magnified in you. Through such comes harmony, joy, peace, and might. (397-1)AR

This result is created when you live this law sincerely from your heart. It then becomes a part of the Law of Love, one of the Laws of Transformation and brings the higher spiritual qualities and experience into expression in your life. If you are in a situation and you are unclear how to apply this law, Freeze-Frame — go to your heart and ask. You will receive an answer that will invoke the higher transformative nature of this law.

Using the Golden Law from the heart creates a movement from the karmic aspect of the law, the Law of Cause and Effect, to a higher level of consciousness. Then we are able to meet the unpleasant karmic conditions that we have created and deal with them without creating more difficulty for ourselves. It gives us a way out, a higher road, a chance to graduate to a higher grade. By it we are blessed with the opportunity to take a major step in our lives — a step to higher consciousness — to transform our lives. That is the power that this law and teaching gives us.

The Golden Law becomes the Law of Mercy (chapter 11) as we apply it by showing mercy to others, particularly to those who err. The mercy we show brings mercy into our lives. We again move from being subject to the Laws of Cause and Effect to a higher state of being — to a greater degree of understanding. It brings us closer to greater oneness with the Divine. That is the result when we sincerely apply the Golden Rule.

CARE

It is easy to acknowledge the Master Law of Relationships and yet not bring it into expression. This teaching has been around for ages, yet it is not strongly manifest in our world today. This may be because there is a great deal of difference between an intellectual understanding of the law and the practical ability to bring it into expression. To make it easier to focus on specific applications, let's explore some simple, practical ways of bringing not only the cause-and-effect aspects of this law into expression—but also the potential transformative aspects that the law holds for us. We can come to know that love expressed in the relationship brings transformation to our relationships and returns to ourselves.

A fundamental quality desired in relationships is care. We want people to sincerely care about and for us. Care is the oil in relationships; it keeps interactions smooth and nonstressful. In his book *Self-Empowerment: The Heart Approach to Stress Management*, Doc Lew Childre points out the great importance of care in our lives.

> Learning to care more sincerely about other people, and yourself, is at the top of the list for efficient self-maintenance. Care regenerates and heals; overcare depletes your energy reserve, often diluting your desire to care any more.
>
> To operate a car without oil in the pistons is equivalent to a human living a life without care in his or her system. True care is a frequency, or feeling, that radiates from your heart. It flows through your system and lubricates your thought and feeling nature, while decreasing friction and resistance in your life. Care not only acts as a mental and emotional detergent within your system, it also adds quality and texture to your relationship with people and all issues.[4]

Bring to mind someone in your life who meant a lot to you. Isn't it someone who sincerely cared about you? Care is the oil that keeps our systems running smoothly. It is important for our internal system, which gets to feel like metal on metal if we do not have ways of expressing care in our life. It is also important for our relationships. If there is no genuine care, they too begin to grate like metal on metal. The answer is to add the oil of care. Care is one of the component frequencies of love. It is a part of the Law of Love. As Cayce put it:

The *joy*, the peace, the happiness, that may be yours comes in doing for others. (262-3)AR

LIGHTNESS

I remember being the recipient of a special moment of care from two friends who showed up at the airport as I was about to board a plane to assist a group that was in conflict. They knew that I found those situations very trying and that I was not looking forward to my experience. Their smiling faces were uplifting, and the feeling of their deep care for me as I faced a challenging assignment encouraged me tremendously. They gave me a small bell on a blue ribbon that I carried with me. It helped me remember to take even the serious situation I was facing with a lightness and the joy of service. That ribbon and bell still hang on my tie rack where it reminds me when I pack for a trip of both the importance of lightness and good friends who are dear to my heart.

That expression of care was a gift which has enriched a friendship and assisted me in that moment and others with the transforming energy of the Law of Love. It is also a picture of the Master Law of Relationships expressed at its highest.

In going through the actions that express care such as: cooking, financial provision, helping with projects at work, listening to a friend, or any of the other thousands of caring activities that can fill our days, it is possible to miss the transformative power of the Law of Love. Love is only present when the feeling of care is there. If the feeling is obligation, resentment, or frustration, ask yourself, is this the way I want others to express care to me? When true balanced care is felt, the activity is energizing and rewarding to the person performing it. That individual is also creating the return into his or her life of the expression of care.

THE SPIRIT OF OUR ACTIONS

The language "*As* you do to others" is used to describe this law because the law goes beyond the physical level. It is not just the what (the act or event) we do that returns to us. That is an oversimplification. A clearer understanding would be that things will be done to us **as** we have done them or **in the same spirit** that we have treated others.

Know the spirit in which you do a thing is the spirit that
will respond to thee! (1688-9)AR

The law operates so that the spirit or intention of an action is
given and received along with that action. An action can convey
a spirit of love, manipulation, hate, peace, understanding, or
joy. That spirit begets the return of actions in that same spirit.

SPIRIT OF A GIFT

For example, let's say that I decided to give a gift to a friend. I
could have many different spirits of expression or motivations
that would make a significant difference in the action. If I felt
under an obligation to buy a gift, I could be resentful of the
money spent and create a transaction of disguised resentment. I
could want to manipulate my friend so that he would feel in-
debted to me, or I could give in love and generosity to enhance
his joy and well-being. The creations I set in motion from these
varying motivations would be very different. In each case, because I had given, I would create a situation of receiving something at a later time. However, what I received could vary, from
gifts that carried resentment or the potential to manipulate me,
to genuine expressions of love and generosity, depending on the
spirit of my giving.

Had I been resentful, I might have received the opportunity to
purchase something at a savings, such as through a distress
sale by a family, where my money was taken reluctantly with
feelings of animosity toward me for profiting at their expense. If
I had been trying to manipulate or ingratiate myself to my friend,
I might be taken out to dinner by a salesperson who did not
really care about me, but simply wanted to make me feel obli-
gated to buy his product. If I gave in a spirit of true love and
generosity, then I would find myself receiving from others in ways
that benefited me without obligation and brought to my awareness the love that others truly held for me. In each case I would
have received in the spirit that I had given. The attitude and the
spirit of our actions are major elements of our creations.

HELPFUL NEIGHBOR

When we look at value given, there are many examples of how
the value begotten or returned is not a monetary value but a

value that is measured by the spirit of the gift. A family in our community had to leave their home, which they were in the process of building, in order to acquire some education the father needed for his work. They were trying to finish the work on their house so it would be easy to live in when they returned. Knowing of their need, a neighbor woman spent considerable time painting without pay just to help her friends through a time that was demanding on them in terms of both time and money. Because of the genuineness of her assistance to her friends, it is easy to imagine that there had also been other times throughout her life when she had extended her support to those around her.

Several years after helping her neighbors, the woman went through a divorce and was without income to meet the needs of herself and her children. The neighbors she had helped and many others assisted her quite freely with money and items from their homes that she could use or sell for money. The monetary value of what she received was greater than the work she did for her friends, but the nature of the giving was the same: others extended themselves to help her unselfishly to the best of their abilities in order to be of real assistance to her through difficult times. What she received in return was not the value of support in terms of dollars. She received genuine assistance, just as she had given.

To teach that lesson, Jesus pointed out to those around Him the example of the woman at the temple who gave the gift of her two mites, which was all she had. Through her giving, He could show His disciples it was not the amount but the spirit of the giving that was important.

The Universal Laws are impartial. They do not reward or punish. They do not try to get us to join a particular religion or hold certain political philosophies. Rather, understanding the law simply assures us that what we create in the lives of others and the spirit with which we bring about that creation will be brought forth into our lives.

TAKING CARE OF SELF

You may find yourself in a relationship where you are sincerely caring for another, but the other person does not respond to the care you are extending. This is not unusual because we all have the ability to accept or reject love, just as we can accept or reject outer gifts. The presence of heartfelt care and wisdom is of great importance for you as you extend it in that relationship, not only because of what it brings the other person but also because it is the most effective way of taking care of yourself.

If someone is not responsive to your care, you may feel anger or resentment, which can be very natural. However, those feelings are the symptoms of overcare and are extremely toxic to your own system. Hormones like adrenaline and cortisol are secreted by the body in those reactions. They age you faster, strain the heart, drain your energy, lower your intelligence, and weaken your immune system. No wonder overcare leaves you feeling drained. Responding from the heart in those situations stops that hormone response and balances the heart rhythms as it takes care of you even if the other person chooses not to respond to your care. These are prime opportunities to do a Freeze-Frame (chapter 5). The return to the heartfelt feeling and the wisdom that is available through your heart guidance brings solution and recharge.

IMMUNE SYSTEM RESPONSE TO FEELINGS AND EMOTIONS

The following test shows what happened to the IgA levels of a group of people who merely remembered being angry for five minutes. IgA is an antibody that is an important part of the immune system. It is the body's first line of defense against colds and flu and an indicator of the overall health of the immune system. The higher the IgA level, the stronger the immune system, or the greater ability the body has to resist colds and flu. After the five minutes of remembering being angry, the people had an initial rise in IgA. Then the IgA level dropped to subnormal levels, and even six hours later the immune system was still depressed. Six hours of lowered immune protection is a high cost for five minutes of just remembering being angry.

In the second test, the people remembered feeling care for five minutes. There is an immediate increase in IgA that is greater than that with anger. Then the IgA level dropped back to normal. During the next six hours it steadily increased. Five minutes of care strengthened the immune system for the next six hours.

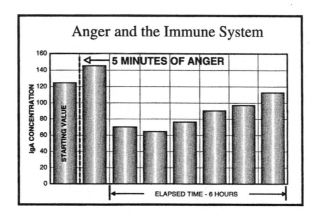

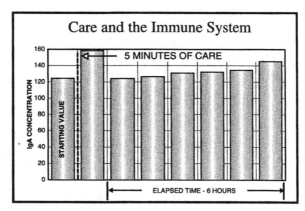

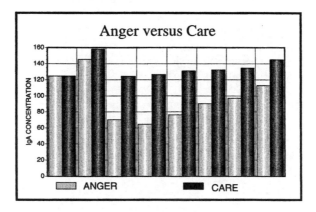

Figures 9A, 9B, 9C

Figs. 9A and 9B illustrate the effect that feeling five minutes of remembered anger or care had on the experimental group's average level of
the immune system antibody IgA throughout the day. There was for both
groups an immediate and significant increase in IgA. With anger, that
dropped to subnormal levels an hour later and stayed subnormal over
the next six hours. With care, the larger initial increase dropped to normal an hour later, but then continued to increase over the next six
hours.[5]

Earlier illustrations demonstrated that appreciation has beneficial effects such as coherent heart frequency patterns, balanced heart rhythms, and the highly efficient result of
entrainment of several biological systems. Figs. 9A and 9B show
that other heartfelt feelings such as care also bring increases in
effective biological functioning to the physical body.

WHO RESPONDS?

When we sincerely care, we receive immediate and longer term
care from our own bodies regardless of other people's responses.
The Golden Law has already worked. What we have done for
another, care, has been done for us. We benefit from the Master
Law of Relationships operating through our bodies to give us
biological care as we extend other forms of care to those in our
lives.
The law does not say that the person to whom you are expressing care will express care to you. It simply provides that
genuine care will be returned to you. This also happens in the
outer sense as well as the biological. The law does not provide
that the return in the outer will be immediate. For my friend
Maria, the return of the care she extended to others came from
different people and at a different time.

MARIA

Maria, a friend of mine for many years, experienced a time
delay of several years before receiving the benefit of actions she
had set in motion. She was a part of a group of friends who had
started a small business together. She believed very much in the
business and what it did for the people of the small community
in which they lived. She put a great deal of time and effort into
the business as her way of caring for others, even though the

financial return to her was minimal. She became the most knowledgeable person about the operation and took on greater and greater responsibility. Many people worked there who had a lesser sense of responsibility and put in less time than Maria. She willingly carried on her activities, because it was her way of providing support for the others. Because of her skill and dedication, many of the people in the community received income and sustenance from the business.

Years later, Maria became interested in traveling to another country to study. The cost of the trip and the expenses of getting established in the other country were considerable, particularly for a person of Maria's modest means. Several people became aware of her desire and offered her financial opportunities and support. That which she had provided to others years before returned to her for her new undertaking.

OVERCARE

If care is energizing, why are relationships sometimes draining? Often giving care to the people we care about most such as our children, parents, or spouse leaves us exhausted because it is very easy to move from care into overcare without knowing it. We began exploring overcare in chapter 6. Overcare occurs when our care, which is energizing, becomes draining. It occurs when we are caring not from the heart but from our insecurities and fears. Overcare is care that is no longer balanced. It is draining because it is either no longer filled with the heart feelings of care or it is contrary to the wisdom of the heart.

Cayce gave this advice with regard to marriage, encouraging both care and avoiding overcare:

> Q. How can I be of greatest help to my present husband?
> A. Disappointments and differences have arisen. Do not *withdraw*, but rather let your associations be as a *loving* indifference. Not mindful of the slights and slurs, yet knowing that indeed and in truth as you sow, so shall you reap—in your relationships with him, as well as his with you. Do to him, under *any* circumstance, as you would have him do to you. (1125-1)AR

In chapter 6 I related the experience of burnout I had from overcaring as a minister. The patterns of overcare I experienced are similar to what many of us experience in our personal relationships as well as our professional lives. I would frequently receive a call to go assist someone, perhaps at the hospital with the family. It was often at the end of a long, busy day. It was a request to give a little more of my time and energy when I had already given a lot. I discovered that those experiences were some of the most draining and some of the most fulfilling and energizing. Why was that? What was the difference? When we understand the Law of Love, we see that there is the potential for any activity to be transformative. The difference for me was whether or not I engaged my heart through the feeling of care. I found that sometimes my self-talk of how tired I was or how I wanted to be home with my family kept me out of my heart. Instead of the deep feelings of care, my service was perfunctory and I would end up drained. I did what my head told me I should do. "It is my responsibility. It's the right thing to do. They need my support." At other times I went to the deep feelings of care in my heart and my system was energized. Even when it was late at night, I went home feeling fulfilled.

I also discovered when I checked my heart that sometimes that wisdom directed me to respond differently than I had intended. Sometimes the direction was not to go at all, to go at a different time, to have someone else involved, to change my attitude, or to interact with the people and situation differently than I expected. These changes and responses were the result of that deeper wisdom of the heart. My heart wisdom was taking care of me as I was taking care of others. This direction from my heart kept me true to the Golden Rule. My heart wisdom assisted me in caring in a balanced way that met my needs as well as others. That is how I would want people to extend care to me.

In each case, the movement of attention from the head to the heart and the activation of the feeling of care brought the change in understanding and attitude. Simply telling myself I should care more or that I needed to enforce a personal boundary did not bring me renewed energy or assist me in meeting the challenge effectively. Whether the change was outer or inner, it had to come from the heart. In the heart the transformative power of the Law of Love is activated.

In these situations we discover the potential of the Master Law of Relationships. If we are doing to others as we would have them do to us, from a purely intellectual response, we will find the law brings us like responses in our life, but they are not fulfilling or transforming. To bring the full power of transformation into the relationship, that which we do for others must come from the heart. Then we and the relationship are transformed.

WORRY

One of the most draining influences on our relationships and ourselves is worry and overcares similar to worry, such as choosing our responses to people because of our concerns about "what they will think." These responses are not from the care within our hearts but from our insecurities. They are draining to our systems and to our relationships as well. Worry does not help us care effectively for another, and we have all experienced how it drains our energy. Yet some of us learned from the patterns in our families or friends that if you cared about someone, you worried about them. A friend I work with was telling me about transforming the overcare of worry which was very strong in her family.

GRANDMOTHER'S WORRY

Angela remembered watching her grandmother at the window when it was time for her grandfather to come home. Her grandmother would sit at the window watching for her husband to come around the corner. If he was even one minute late, she would begin to ring her hands and say things like, "I wonder if something has happened to him. I wonder if he is all right. What if he is hurt." As a granddaughter, Angela wanted to assure her grandmother that things were okay. She had observed that Grandfather was often late, but he always arrived safely.

As an adult, Angela noticed that she tended to worry about things. She worried about her assignments at work and many other elements in her life. Looking back at her life, she realized that her mother, who was an only child, grew up in the household where Angela's grandmother worried constantly. The grandmother had immigrated to this country, did not communicate easily, and had experienced a crippling illness so that she was very dependent on her husband. It was easy to understand why she had the insecurities that were behind her worries. Angela's mother had a secure loving childhood, but she had been around the worries so much that she had developed the pattern of worrying as well, even though hers was less than the grandmother's.

Angela, like her mother, had acquired the habit of worry from being raised in a household where the adults consistently expressed that attitude. Angela recognized that the worry was part of the overcare that hindered her work and kept the fun and fulfillment out of her life. She began to transform the pattern of overcare within her by using Cut-Thru.

CUT-THRU

Cut-Thru is a technique that brings the transforming impact of the Law of Love to overcares. It is very effective with deeply ingrained emotional patterns such as worry which are encoded in our system at a cellular level. Angela experienced that encoding after she had been using Cut-Thru. She told me she had used Cut-Thru on her worrisome thoughts and feelings. Now she almost never worries. The patterns that she "inherited" from her mother and grandmother seemed to be eliminated from her system. She felt free of them until she noticed one day that she was sitting very tense at her computer. Her body was tensing just as it used to when she would worry. She realized that this was a cellular response pattern in her body. Her body continued to react as though she were worrying. She went back to using Cut-Thru and soon eliminated the pattern of body tension as well.

In chapter 3, I gave an example of the overcares I experienced about meeting people and of how Cut-Thru had freed me from those patterns. The reason Cut-Thru is so effective is that it applies the Law of Love. The love energy of the heart is used to transform the patterns we are experiencing without our having to bring up a lot of past memories or analyze the experience.

The steps of Cut-Thru are progressive. You use each step until you get relief. At that point you skip the rest of the steps and switch to the fifth and final step. Cut-Thru can be used in a few minutes' time, or it can be used over twenty to thirty minutes when you have that longer period of time available.

Because Cut-Thru is one of the most effective methods I have found to apply the Law of Love, I am including the steps of Cut-Thru here for your use. These steps are very carefully designed to utilize specific aspects of the love energy that flows through the heart. I strongly encourage you to get Doc Lew Childre's book CUT-THRU and work with his directions in applying these steps to your overcares.[6] (Planetary Publications, P.O. Box 66, Boulder

Creek, CA 95006, or phone 800-372-3100) When we lower the ratio of overcare in our life, the Golden Law and the Law of Love together bring into our lives the fulfilling relationships that are our heart's desire.

STEPS OF CUT-THRU®

Step 1. Recognize feelings and thoughts of overcare—Take an inner weather report. See if your inner weather is rain or sunshine. Then change your weather to prevent a flood. Choose the more hopeful perspective.

Step 2. Hold overcare thoughts or feelings in the heart. Remember, adapting stops the energy drain. Pretend you are floating on a raft or soaking in a heart-warming bath for a few minutes. If the disturbed feelings won't release or if your emotions are really revved up, homogenizing or blending the feelings in the heart helps the energy disperse so that you can see a new perspective.

Step 3. Find your peace. As the current of discomfort dissipates, a new sense of peace and intuitive knowing can emerge. Hold to any feeling of peace. Then go to the "fair heart" to see and reflect clearly.

Step 4. Find the reference point of care. Ask yourself, "Why did I originally care?" Recall those beginning feelings of care for a few moments. Then ask yourself, "How did my original care slowly leak away due to overcare, and drain me?" Recognize how your care was taken to inefficient extremes. Recall the original care and find the higher heart perspective.

Step 5. Follow your heart intelligence. In this last step, with clear perception and feelings of sincerity coming back, listen to your heart to know what *true care* would now be in this situation. Follow your true care. That's caring for self and others.[7]

This internal process is so powerful in its transformative effect that researchers discovered startling results in a study of a group of people who used this method regularly along with the music *Speed of Balance* by Doc Lew Childre.[8] This study found that after daily use of Cut-Thru and the music for a month, the levels of the hormone DHEA increased an average of 100 percent. This hormone is called the vitality hormone or the anti-aging hormone. Many people, recognizing the health effects of DHEA, attempt to increase their levels through other sources. Cut-Thru uses only the Law of Love and is far more effective. The study also proved that there was a decrease of the stress hormone cortisol by twenty-three percent, a significant and important drop.[9]

LISTENING AND SPEAKING FROM THE HEART

"Words which come from the heart enter the heart."
Moses Iben Ezra

One of the finest combinations of the Golden Law and the Law of Love is the experience of listening and speaking from your heart to another. We want to be heard, and we really want to hear what others have to say to us. The difficulty is that our head takes the information and forms perceptions of what this communication is about, and we begin to prepare our answer. How do we bring a higher transformative level of communication to our relationships? Not through the head. Telling ourselves we should listen better doesn't do it because the head cannot manage the head.

If we move our attention to the area of our hearts and feel our care about what the person is saying—really feel that love and care—then the heart can keep us listening. As mentioned briefly in chapter 6, it is almost as though you listen through your heart. You cannot interrupt internally or externally, and you can allow the person to complete communication with your full, receptive, caring attention. If you take a moment then to reflect back on what you heard—noting even deeper essence levels of the communication that may have come to your heart—you have made a heart connection between two people.

The next step is to speak from your heart. That is different than the "telling our truth" I hear most people talking about. What I experience when many people tell their truth is "dumping their stuff." It isn't even what they really want to communicate, because it is mixed up with a bunch of emotions they are processing, and it comes across as attack, anger, frustration, rejection, etc. What they really wanted to do was sincerely tell the other person of a concern or thought they had. People have important things to communicate. Speaking from your heart allows the emotionally difficult, the ordinary, and the wonderful things in our lives to be communicated and received.

Before speaking, do a quick Freeze-Frame. Focus on your heart. With your heart energy active, speak sincerely to the other person. Say what is really on your heart. The heart power of the Law of Love transforms the emotional energy and moves it into sincerity. When the person you are speaking to hears your sincerity, he or she can usually receive your message. You have then put these two laws to work in your relationship. Apply a dose of patience, and you will find the results are transformative.

Chapter 10

The Law of Faith

Whatever you ask in prayer, you will receive if you have faith.
Jesus   (Matthew 21:22)

One of the most powerful experiences of the Laws of Transformation is the experience that seems to suspend the natural laws. We suddenly witness another realm of law in action and want to call it a miracle. Many such experiences are sudden healings or demonstrations of prosperity or similar events that were totally unexpected in the normal course of events.

I have a friend who showed me a ring manifested for him by an Eastern teacher who reached into the air and produced this very unique ring that fit him perfectly. My friend took the ring and had it analyzed. The results puzzled the analysts because there appeared to be elements in the ring of which they had no knowledge. Jesus fed a group of people comprised of 5,000 men, which means that including women and children there were probably close to 10,000 people. He did this by praying over five loaves of bread and two fish. Another friend of mine was passing through a children's hospital when he experienced a strong urge to pray with a little boy. He asked the mother if he could, and she approved so he prayed with the boy. Several days later he learned that the boy's illness had been diagnosed as terminal, but it had disappeared that day and the child was soon released from the hospital.

What was the secret these people knew? They produced instantaneous physical responses to their desires. For that to happen, there must be some lawful way to bring about such changes. To understand the process that these people and countless others have used to manifest their requests of Spirit into the world, one must understand the Law of Faith, one of the Laws of Transformation.

The Law of Faith—"Inner asking plus inner knowing results in manifestation."

We can also express the Law of Faith in the words that Jesus used to teach it: "Whatever you ask in prayer, you will receive, if you have faith." (Matthew 21:22 RSV)

The conditions of this law, asking and knowing, become major factors in our ability to bring the qualities of life that we desire into expression. "Knowing" in this law is not head knowledge or mere belief. It is a heart knowledge. "Knowing" is an inner experience that Jesus called faith. This deep inner change of awareness—"knowing"— that activates this law is very different from the experience that most people think of when they mention faith.

When someone speaks of faith, he or she usually means a set of beliefs—the Catholic faith, the Baptist faith, or the Muslim faith. Sometimes they are talking about how fervently or strongly someone believes, such as, "He has a lot of faith." In this law, belief is only a small part of the experience. The law actually operates through energy that is released through an experience we sometimes try to describe as "knowing." Belief can help us get to knowing.

THE CONFUSION OF BELIEF

In many instances the Law of Faith is the cause of the kind of phenomenon mentioned above. However, this law is one of the most misunderstood of the Laws of Transformation. The reason for this is that it has been described in terms of belief and associated with Jesus' teaching:

Believe that you have received it, and it will be yours. Mark 11:24 (NIV)

Another association that has confused our understanding of

this law is His teaching, "Ask and it will be given unto you." As a result of this language people have thought that if they believed something strong enough, it would come true, or if they prayed to Jesus, they would get what they prayed for. This has happened for some people, and we point to and present those instances as a law at work. People for whom this did not happen were sometimes told they did not believe enough or have enough faith. This is not necessarily true at all because many other elements and laws are involved in the process of manifestation.

I have also had personal experiences of being cured of illness, being involved in cures for other individuals, and witnessing demonstrations that were beyond any natural law I could identify. I can look objectively at those experiences and state that my faith was not as strong as those friends who did not find themselves cured or did not have a needed manifestation take place. I had more doubt and more questions and was surprised at the outcome again and again. Yet the healing happened in my life but not in theirs. While faith or belief is a truly valuable and important element in one's life, it can be very misunderstood in terms of saying we are going to receive something simply because of the depth of our belief. In many experiences, such as serious illness, there are other laws involved of which one of the most powerful is the overriding influence of the soul's blueprint through the Law of Choice.

A popular teaching states that "whatever you believe and can conceive you can achieve." This is an inspirational admonition, but it is not so as a matter of law. Belief and conceptualization are powerful influences that are valuable aspects of a successful endeavor. However, they alone do not assure the outcome. There are Universal Laws relating to belief, but they do not provide that we will receive something solely on the strength of our belief. Fortunately, we can also have wonderful experiences that we did not really believe possible. I once figured out that I was constantly being blessed beyond what I really believed possible. Fortunately for my life, belief was not a prerequisite. It seemed to me that God believed in me even though I was very reluctant to fully return the compliment.

Although belief is an important element in our prayer demonstrations, we cannot turn to belief or conceptualization as the sole operative mechanism of the transformative power that is associated with faith. Let's examine how transformative experiences are a part of what we can call faith.

A NEED FOR MONEY

I experienced the transformative power of the Law of Faith some years ago when I had run out of money. My wife and I lived in a rural area of Montana and needed our jeep to get around the muddy roads. The jeep was in the shop where it had been repaired, but we had no money to pay for it. The shop called and asked us to come pick it up. Frustrated with the lack of money, I went into my room to pray. Understanding intellectually that God is the source of and supplies all that we need and that there is always abundant supply, I tried to turn to that source.

After extensive arguments with God, self-criticisms, and doubts that preceded my more frustrated prayers, I turned to the understanding that God is love. I allowed myself to feel loved and could then remember many experiences of being loved by others and of having the clear sense of God's love for me. After this, I managed to achieve some measure of inner stillness. From there I experienced a great sense of peace and released the frustrations, questions, doubts, and worries that I had been carrying. I experienced a deep sense of assurance—a "knowing"—that the problem was taken care of, although I had no idea how.

I went outside and told my wife that I knew that everything was being taken care of. Being a very patient and understanding soul she smiled at me, said "good," and went back to her work. I was so sure of that perception that several hours later I got in my car and started to drive into town to pick up the jeep even though I had no money. As I was pulling out of our quarter-mile-long driveway, a car pulled up and a lady from a town sixty miles away rolled down her window and handed me a check. She said she had an urgent feeling that I needed this. She turned her car around and drove the hour back to town. The check, of course, was the amount of the repair bill on the jeep, plus enough for a tank of gas. "Inner asking plus inner knowing brings manifestation."

A HEART CONNECTION

When we look at this experience to see how the law worked, there are several elements that tell us a lot about the law. The first is that it was not my belief that made it work. I did not believe someone would give me money. I did not know what to do except pray. I did not turn to prayer because I thought I could pray and get the money. I turned to prayer because I was feeling so much internal stress that I did not know how else to get relief. What I had was not faith but hope and a belief that I could have a relationship with God. My belief pointed me to prayer. My hope was that there would be a response to my need whether it was help with the car situation or just assistance with the internal stress I was feeling. Hope, even in small amounts, is tremendously important, because it gives us the energy to take a fresh action.

The point at which I experienced another type of energy at work was when I had the feeling of being loved. This was a change of frequency within my being. I felt the dissolution of my concern and the uplifting energy of my heart being filled with the feeling of love. At that point, I had my "knowing"— my inner experience in which I was aware it was taken care of.

With our current knowledge of the heart, we now know that it is at the point of experiencing a core heart feeling such as love that transformation occurs in the biological and electromagnetic system. With that change is the activation of another level of intelligence—the intelligence of the heart. That intelligence is an entirely different domain of intelligence than what we experience through the intellect. This intuitive intelligence is capable of interacting with and utilizing data beyond what is available though the five senses.

In my experience, the change of frequency from the worrisome thoughts of my head to the heart frequency of love activated my ability to deal with this situation from another level of intelligence. It was apparently in that moment that a cooperative connection was made with the lady who was willing to be supportive of me by giving the gift of the money. I knew that there was a response to my need although I did not know the nature of that response. It was not that I had faith in it because I had prayed; it was that I had a knowingness of it being dealt with because I had experienced the solution at a level beyond my conscious recognition.

CHANGING HOLOGRAMS

Another way to describe this experience would be to say I had changed the hologram in which I was operating. A hologram is a three-dimensional image. Many properties of the creation of a hologram are analogous to the way we create our reality, both perceived and manifest.

In the experience of "knowing," the individual makes the connection with the spiritual energy that enters through the heart. In my experience above, I made that connection when I felt and accepted the love. The biophysiological changes that take place at that state are a physical expression of changes that are taking place at other levels of my being. The spiritual energy entering the system is activating a different aspect of the individual's soul blueprint—a new hologram. Because of my intention to deal with the lack of money for the car, a hologram wherein I had enough money for the car was activated. Since we are all linked in that spiritual energy field, the woman who was willing to support me in that hologram received her "knowing" and she acted upon it.

There are many possible holograms we could be living. They are the movies we are producing, acting in, and directing. Which movie do you want? The one you are in is the one you have chosen at present. If you want a different movie—a different hologram—how do you create it? It takes both asking and the inner connection with your heart intelligence where you **know** that hologram is being activated.

The potential of the hologram you desire is contained within the frequencies and intelligence stored in your heart crystals. The deep, sincere connection with the core frequencies of your heart sets up the coherence in the electromagnetic system (see fig. 3C) where the spiritual energy necessary to activate those heart crystals can enter the system. The energy is directed by you through your asking. Once the heart crystals are stimulated through the spiritual energy, the holographic shift can occur. That is when the knowingness takes place. The "knowing" is your intuitive awareness of the new hologram.

Although there are many pieces of this process that are not yet provable in the lab, there are some scientific pieces of evidence in place supporting parts of this understanding. In her book *The Hidden Power of the Heart*, Sara Paddison describes the way coherence in the heart (fig. 3C) facilitates the cascade of higher dimensional energy into our system without the loss of the knowledge carried by the wave form. It is like a radio receiver that has a clear connection so that you can hear distinctly the music or words it carries instead of one that is distorted by static. She cites research from the Institute of HeartMath and Daniel Winter that shows the ratio of the wave peaks in the heart electromagnetic spectrum is 1.618, the ratio of the Golden Mean which is the most efficient ratio for energy to cascade down a series without losing power or geometry. This is also the ratio of our DNA structure.[1]

LOVE AND DNA

An interesting experiment demonstrates a relationship between coherence in the heart (feelings of love) and our DNA. The experiment was the attempt to see if intention (asking) could affect our DNA. Several samples were tested. The senders of the instruction to the DNA were monitored for their heart spectrum readout. The object was to see if by intention one could make the DNA wind or unwind. DNA naturally winds and unwinds although it is quite stable at room temperature.

The senders concentrated on intending their samples of DNA to either wind or unwind. The control sample did not attempt to change their DNA over the duration of the experiment.

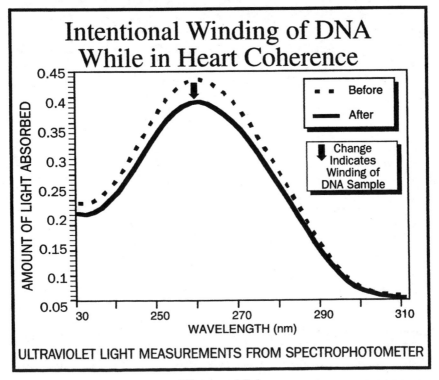

Figure 10A

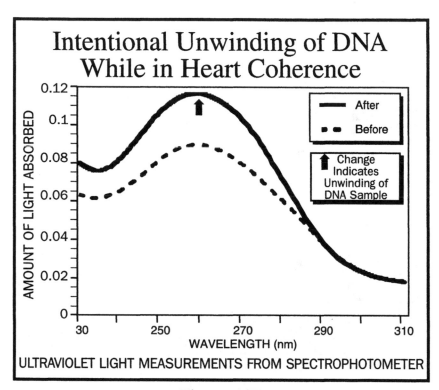

Figure 10B

Figs. 10A and 10B are the result of experiments in which the winding and unwinding of DNA was measured by a spectrophotometer. The results occurred in response to intentional direction from subjects whose heart electricities were coherent. The winding intention resulted in the DNA winding; the unwinding intention resulted in the DNA unwinding. Where the heart electricities were not coherent, no intentional effect was measured.[2]

As shown in the above graphs, the sample the sender intended to wind, did wind. In response to the sender's conscious intention for the DNA to unwind, the sample did unwind. However, not everyone could replicate the experiment. The response of intentional direction of the winding or unwinding of the DNA **only took place when the sender was in a deeply felt core heart feeling**, shown by the coherent frequency spectrum from the ECG monitor. Without that focus of sincere heart feeling, the sender could not intentionally alter the DNA.

What the experiment shows us is that our heart feelings connect us through the heart to a major communication system that can bring our intention into effect on the very blueprint of our cells. When we see the connection possible through the heart, the ability of the Law of Faith to bring about major changes in our lives begins to lose some of the mystical and mysterious aspects that have clothed its function. It becomes as it always was, a lawful process of transformation.

MYRTLE FILLMORE'S HEALING

A woman by the name of Myrtle Fillmore dealt with the Law of Faith when she was in the final stages of terminal tuberculosis. Doctors had informed her long ago that they held no hope for her and could only use their medical knowledge to chart unerringly the path of her demise.

Myrtle had long been a spiritual student and, like any earnest seeker, had explored many paths and understandings of the Divine. Yet in one particular moment, a statement she heard about her relationship to God took on a totally different meaning for her. The teaching, "You are a child of God and therefore you do not inherit sickness," was suddenly illumined within her understanding in such a way that she "knew" it was true. She had passed beyond the mental or intellectual level of perception and from the spiritual received this new self-perception as a true, realized fact.

She had the knowingness of that truth but not of her healing. She received an intuitive understanding that she could consciously direct the cells of her body and that they would respond to that direction. She then utilized that intuitive intelligence to set about changing the hologram for her body. She sat down and consciously addressed her body organs, apologizing for her limiting thoughts and acknowledging the new understanding she had gained that they were perfect channels of God-life expressing. She did this daily for over two years, resulting in the total elimination of all disease from her physical body.

Let's look at her description of the words she used in that process. From the above experiment we know that only the intentions from one who is centered in heart love can intentionally alter the DNA. Do you hear that love in her words?

I told the life in my liver that it was not torpid or inert, but full of vigor and energy. I told the life in my stomach that it was not weak or inefficient, but energetic, strong, and intelligent. I told the life in my abdomen that it was no longer infested with ignorant ideas of disease, put there by myself and by doctors, but that it was all athrill with the sweet, pure, wholesome energy of God. I told my limbs that they were active and strong. I told my eyes that they did not see of themselves but that they expressed the sight of Spirit, and that they were drawing on an unlimited source. I told them that they were young eyes, clear, bright eyes, because the light of God shone right through them. I told my heart that the pure life of Jesus Christ flowed in and through its beatings and that all the world felt its joyous pulsation.

I went to all the life centers in my body and spoke words of Truth to them—words of strength and power. I asked their forgiveness for the foolish, ignorant course that I had pursued in the past when I had condemned them and called them weak, inefficient, and diseased. I did not become discouraged at their being slow to wake up, but kept right on, both silently and aloud, declaring the words of Truth, until the organs responded. And neither did I forget to tell them that they were free, unlimited Spirit. I told them that they were no longer in bondage to the carnal mind; that they were not corruptible flesh, but centers of life and energy omnipresent.

Then I asked the Father to forgive me for taking His life into my organism and there using it so meanly. I promised Him that I would never, never again retard the free flow of that life through my mind and my body by any false word or thought; that I would always bless it and encourage it with true thoughts and words in its wise work of building my body temple; that I would use all diligence and wisdom in telling it just what I wanted it to do.

I also saw that I was using the life of the Father in thinking thoughts and speaking words, and I became very watchful as to what I thought and said.

I did not let any worried or anxious thoughts into my mind and I stopped speaking gossipy, frivolous, petulant, angry words. I let a little prayer go up every hour that Jesus Christ would be with me and help me to think and speak only kind, loving, true words; and I am sure that He is with me, because I am so peaceful and happy now. Myrtle Fillmore[3]

Myrtle applied the Law of Faith. The law does not say that
what we know will manifest instantaneously. With her "knowing" came a connection with her heart intelligence that gave
direction for Myrtle to follow in bringing her knowing into manifestation. She utilized the directions she received from her inner
experience to carry out the process of building the relationship
with God that she had been shown in order to bring into the
reality of her physical body the resulting vibrant health.

ELLIE

The diagnosis of cancer had hit Ellie hard. She was young and
in the midst of leaving her nursing career to become a minister.
She had heard of other people having to use their spiritual
knowledge to bring about healing, but she never thought it would
apply to her. After the diagnosis of malignancy, she started her
inner work of prayer and self-examination.

She went through the first operation, and it was a success, as
far as it went. However, the cancer was in a difficult location and
the doctors had not been able to get it all. They scheduled another operation so they could get what they hoped was the rest
of it. She returned to her inner work of finding her source of
healing. She looked deep within to try to find that which was
whole—the spiritual part of herself. Through her own effort, her
own desire, she was able to turn her mind from her body, her
illness, and the fears and concerns that she was carrying, and
consciously became aware of the spiritual part of her own being.

Afterward, when she described her experience to me, she said
that she became powerfully aware right at that moment that she
was whole. She had an experience of her own wholeness and
knew that she was whole and well, regardless of what happened
to her body. She spoke without any trace of fear when she said
that she would experience peace even if her body died, because
she knew that she was not her body and that she was whole.

Ellie experienced her true self. It was a direct experience of
her divine or spiritual nature. Ellie's awareness had shifted fully
from identification with the body to identification with that part
of her that animated the body and would exist long after the
body was gone.

This is an experience of faith. It was a knowingness of the
divine presence, or as faith has been called by another spiritual
teacher, the awareness of the creator in the creation. It is, as it

was for Ellie, experiential in nature. It results not in intellectual ideas but in a realization or knowingness about one's self. This is one of the meanings of faith. Not a thought or a belief but an experience from which one knows deep within one's true nature.

Ellie also utilized the tools of loving herself and prayer in bringing the experience of wholeness into her body. She understood how to meet the inner patterns she found. It was through her work in facing self-rejecting patterns, loving herself, and forgiving others that she utilized the power of knowingness she had received.

Ellie's healing could have taken many forms. It could have been a successful operation, the discovery of a new drug, years of gradually improving health as it was for Myrtle Fillmore, or if her own soul purpose was complete, it could have been the release of her body. For Ellie it was the discovery when the operation took place that the cancer was already gone from her body.

Ellie's experience offers us a look into the experience of faith. The seeking within the self to find one's true nature sets up the experience. It is often difficult for people to describe what they find there. But it was this power to perceive and experience the true pattern or higher hologram within us that Jesus spoke of when He taught the Law of Faith, "Whatever you ask in prayer, you will receive it if you have faith."

All types of faith lead toward manifestation. Each type of faith experience involves a kind of knowing that results from contact with the heart intelligence. The manifestation takes place to the degree that contact opens the individual for the influx of the spiritual energy sufficient to make the shift of holograms.

IDENTITY

Ellie's experience illustrates a direct experience of her spiritual self. She became aware, not that she was going to be healed, but that she was whole. She entered into total identification with her spiritual self. She not only received the revelation of her true nature, but she was able to experience that nature. She shifted into another dimension of her being through the power of her heart. For that time she lived in the other hologram as her reality. When she returned her attention to the old hologram, the wholeness of the spiritual self was manifest.

REVELATION

Another type of faith experience occurs when an individual receives a deep revelation of his or her relationship to the Divine and yet does not enter into identity with that part of him/herself. Myrtle Fillmore's healing appears to have involved this kind of experience of faith. She was able to know that she was a child of God and understood from that that she did not inherit sickness. Her inner experience resulted in that revelation filling her mind so that she "knew" that relationship to be the truth. It was dimensionally different than intellectually realizing the statement was true. The intellectual realization would not have had a transformational impact.

RELEASE

This type of faith experience involves the individual seeking resolution of a problem through inner asking or prayer and experiencing the release of the worry, concern, and limiting beliefs associated with the problem. This is what occurred with me and the need for money. This is not the experience of revelation where the understanding of limiting perception is revealed and the true relationship given, as happened for Myrtle, and no sense of identity with the Divine nature has taken place as with Ellie. Yet the individual has connected with the energy and intelligence of the heart and experienced, at a level that is not conscious, a hologram in which the solution is real, thus knowing that the problem has been handled.

ASKING

Having looked at the dynamic of faith, which is the mechanism Jesus described for the operation of this law, the other element is "inner asking." Asking is a necessary step in the operation of this law. The reason for asking is that the greater goodness being sought has not yet manifested. When something has not manifested, it is usually because the consciousness of the person is not fully open to receive what is desired. The person has not mastered that frequency within him- or herself. The problem is not that God would withhold anything from a person. What we are seeking is already available on the spiritual level, but we have not yet attuned ourselves to receive it at the mental, emotional, and physical levels. The asking is a way to direct ourselves to move beyond any blocks and attune to the hologram in which what we want is a reality. We are not asking God to give us something, for God has no limits on giving. We are acknowledging God as our source, while asking our spiritual nature or heart intelligence to help us become receptive.

Only an inward asking, such as prayer, works every time as a matter of law. Asking of the world assures us of nothing. Only when we ask of our divine nature have we turned our attention to that which is the source of the transformation we are seeking. It does not matter if it is wisdom, healing, abundance, or a change in a relationship; the divine presence can help us open to what is sought when we ask.

The asking and knowing bring manifestation. They do not produce it immediately; rather, they lay before us the way to attune to the frequency band of the hologram we wish to manifest. Myrtle Fillmore's way of attuning was through the heartfelt instruction of the cells of her body. Ellie's was through continuing her process of affirmation and emotional healing. My attunement was through waiting until instructed by my intuition to go and then being receptive to the offered gift. In listening to the guidance from our intuition, we are making the adjustments to allow the hologram to manifest fully in the three-dimensional world.

Many people, immediately following the inner experience, return to their old head pattern and their old way of thinking and do not continue attuning to the guidance that is helping them unfold the new hologram. I remember hearing of a man who received a healing from a spiritual healer. He was experiencing the hologram of his wholeness, completely manifest. His comment was that it probably would not last. Of course it did not. Staying healthy was not a frequency he was willing to accept as reality. Many people have been given guidance on how to manifest a spiritual insight—a new hologram for themselves; however, it meant changing the way they thought and acted. Myrtle had to give up the pity and drama of dying and take the time for what probably seemed like a ridiculous action to any educated person of her day—talking to her cells.

There is a limit on our ability to affect other people through our own internal experience. We cannot control another to make that person respond to us in a certain way. We cannot force others to change as we want them to or as we believe is best for them. They have the power to determine their own response. However, we can support them in entering into a new hologram if they are willing to be receptive.

HEALING OF A CHILD

I experienced this interaction with another person when my oldest daughter, Lisa, was about five years old. I was a single parent and cared very deeply about her well-being. One night she was very sick, and I was unable to get her fever down. It was very late at night, and she could not sleep from her discomfort even though she was exhausted. I had read about the power of prayer, but I had had no experience of it healing someone. However, it was the only recourse left which in my life has often been the point at which I turn to God. I concentrated on sincere prayer for her healing. I went over the words of asking. I felt no change, simply my heart desire for her well-being. Then I became silent and with strong concentration and care directed a flow of energy from my heart to my daughter. This lasted for probably fifteen minutes. I felt a sense of relief and completion. I did not know its full effect on her, but she had in that time finally fallen asleep and was resting comfortably for the first time in many hours. The flush of the fever was gone from her cheeks and though warm, she no longer felt feverish.

We had experienced many sicknesses in her early years. They all ended the same, with a gradual recovery and then at least a day or more until she returned to her full energy and vigor. That next morning, early, she bounded into my room as though she had been perfectly healthy the night before and had just awakened from a good, long night's sleep.

She was receptive, and I was able to support the change of hologram for her through the energy of my heart. As I look at that experience, it was not my asking that brought the change in frequency. My asking brought an intuitive sense of what to do that would be supportive of her change to the hologram of wholeness. As I did that, I felt the flow of heart energy which was quite tangible. It was also very clear to me when that was complete. The knowing in this case, much like Myrtle's, was the understanding of how to proceed and the sense of the reality of what was taking place, instead of writing it off as a silly idea or wishful thinking.

We can pray and send that spiritual energy successfully in

support of another. The process of sending that support through the heart is very important. It is now the most satisfying way for me to support my children. Lisa is now married and a graduate student on the other side of the country. I cannot be at her bedside in time of sickness or when she has to make the challenging decisions that are a part of her world. I can send that deep love from my heart in support of the next hologram she is reaching for in her life. I can also often feel when my mother is doing the same for me. In this world of mobility that places us at great distances from each other, I am grateful for the Law of Faith, because I know that my inner asking guides me to that point where inner knowing takes place. That is the connection which supports, but does not compel, the manifestation of the highest hologram possible in the lives of those I love.

THE MASTER LAW OF TRANSFORMATION

He who worships me with unfaltering love transcends those gunas.[4] He becomes fit to reach union with Brahman. For I am Brahman within this body, Life immortal That shall not perish: I am the Truth and the Joy for ever.
Bhagavad Gita[5]

... you will know the truth, and the truth will set you free.   Jesus   (John 8:32 NIV)

The Law of Truth—"Know the Truth and the Truth will set you free."

All the Laws of Transformation are dynamics that give expression to this master law. The Law of Truth is about "knowing" as we have seen it applied in the Law of Faith. It is the experience of the spiritual self. It is not a concept or understanding, but rather the experience of that self. The freedom it brings is from limiting patterns within our consciousness. These patterns keep us from expressing the power and beauty of our true nature.

We have also explored another of the fundamental laws of transformation, the Law of Love, "Love transforms." In this law, the love itself is the experience of knowing. God is love, so to love is to be in contact with and to be an expression of that divine presence. The transformation is the release of the limiting pattern as a higher one is created.

These laws are the instruments through which we can constantly transform our lives.

The spirit of truth is nigh unto you . . . seek him in your
own heart . . . (5752-5)AR

Chapter 11

Attunement Through Mercy and Balance

We have been examining Laws of Transformation which bring transformation into our lives moment by moment. They also serve another function in our growth. They plug us into the divine wisdom and help us uplift our creation to a new level.

Sustaining that new creation in its higher purpose and direction is the role of another set of laws—the Universal Laws of Attunement. They operate to keep us attuned to and receptive to the flow of higher intelligence and energy that sustains the harmony of our creation.

The following laws—the Laws of Mercy, Balance, Enlightenment, One, and Becoming—are Laws of Transformation, but they are also Laws of Attunement. As you live them, they will bring such reorientation and connection to your life that you will become a force for the manifestation of the divine purpose in your world.

The Law of Mercy—"If you would have mercy, show mercy."

Whenever you use mercy, you are employing the full power that love can exert to change or transform whatever situation you are involved in. How do we give mercy? According to the readings, mercy is a quality we can employ in our relations with others under two very different sets of circumstances. These two extremes in life which test your true colors in applying mercy are two of the toughest tests you are ever likely to face:

- The first: When you have someone in your power or under your control or influence and he or she is in opposition to you or has said or done something which you object to, the question is: Can you be merciful to them?
- The second—and toughest test of all: In a situation the reverse of the above, when you are subject to someone else, dominated by them or in their control, and they are mistreating you, the question again is: Can you be merciful to them?

What do these situations require of you? This reading shows a close tie between showing mercy and being able to forgive:

If your will then is one with His, there may come into your experiences the ability to forgive those who have *purposely* wronged you. For your prayer may not approach the throne of mercy unless you have shown mercy to even those that have wronged you in their might or power. (1435-1)AR

That makes sense. As long as we feel we have been ill treated, misused, or wronged, we certainly do not feel like being kind and forgiving (merciful) to that individual. To change that attitude we need to truly forgive that person.

MERCY AS A HIGHER LAW

The readings refer to a Law of Mercy that is clearly a higher law than that dealing only with cause and effect. They indicate that as you become aware of, accept, or begin to turn to that Presence within, you come under the Law of Mercy as well as the Laws of Cause and Effect. This means that by your action of accepting the presence of a higher power within, you come under the mercy of that higher power and that you therefore are living under a different set of rules, a higher dimension of consciousness that enables you to meet your karma with mercy instead of with the normal reaction you might have had previously. When you make this shift in consciousness to accept the higher power within, you see your karma in a different way. You have come under mercy. As the readings put it:

For He has forgiven you already. (262-81)

This realization then makes it easy for you to do likewise and to forgive those with whom you are involved. As we learn to forgive, to release our judgments and resentments of others, we are able to extend mercy, and through that simple act, this marvelous law is invoked.

JUSTICE OR MERCY AS A PERSONAL CHOICE

I was once faced with having to make a decision based on this law. I had been studying the Cayce readings for some years, and I kept being brought back to the understanding that I would become what I focused my mind upon. At the time I was a successful attorney. I even had the "good guy" role—I was fighting to protect the environment and consumer rights. This was a popular position in the press at the time so I received a lot of encouraging publicity. However, I perceived my actions in another light. I looked at them in terms of the Cayce readings. What would I become if I put my mind on the law for the years ahead of me?

I realized that the ultimate I could embody as a lawyer was justice. Even if I kept the concepts of public service in my career, it would enable me to manifest a high degree of justice. That was a noble goal. However, I had been taking a very deep look within myself. I had been learning about the Universal Laws. The Laws of Cause and Effect are laws of justice. Through the Laws of Cause and Effect, the actions, beliefs, thoughts, and feelings we hold return to us. Our lives are the out-picturing of these things. We are learning by meeting ourselves—our creation—each day.

I knew a great deal about myself. Spirit gave me the gift of remembering many lives in the earth. I remembered clearly what I had created and what I had lived through in my learning. I had seen the karmic laws turn what the Buddhists call the endless wheel of birth and death. I knew it intimately. I knew I did not want justice. I did not want to meet my creations because the love in them was small; the ignorance, fear, and selfishness were great.

I looked at what had made the difference in those ages I had walked the earth. The difference was that there were those who did not bring me justice, but instead brought to me the experience of mercy. Those experiences stood out like beacons of light in the storm-tossed sea of karma. The gift of mercy. It was through the mercy of the hearts of many that I was helped to begin anew, to care for others, to find the delight in the goodness that flows through the world and is the world if we will let it in. I do not want to bring justice to any person. Yet I am grateful, if I can return a small portion of the mercy that I received. Do not misunderstand me. This is not a guilt trip over past sins. It is an honest look at how we are in bondage to our ignorance and how love lifts us above that ignorance into fulfillment and meaning.

I left the practice of law because I could not reach for the fullness of mercy as I understood it. That is not to say that there are not lawyers who are true instruments of mercy in the earth, for there are, and I have been honored to meet some of them. It simply was not my way to accomplish that goal. I entered a work that taught people about their hearts and the great Laws of Transformation that lifted them from the justice they were in to the freedom of which their hearts dreamed. I can honestly say that as I have walked this path, I have received in love and mercy far, far more than I have ever given out. I share this beautiful law with you because it is not of cause and effect. You will not get back the mercy and love you give out. You will get a thousand times more.

THE LAW OF BALANCE

Under heaven all can see beauty as beauty only because
   there is ugliness.
All can know good as good only because there is evil.

Therefore having and not having arise together.
Difficult and easy complement each other.
Long and short contrast each other;
High and low rest upon each other;
Voice and sound harmonize each other;
Front and back follow one another.

Therefore the sage goes about doing nothing, teaching no-
   talking.
The ten thousand things rise and fall without cease,
Creating, yet not possessing,
Working, yet not taking credit.
Work is done, then forgotten.

Therefore it lasts forever.

Lao Tsu[1]

The Law of Balance—"All interchanges balance."

A group of women discussing some men who had obviously not bothered to work with the law of balance provided me with perhaps the clearest insight into the law of balance. They observed of the first, "He's so physical, he's boring"; of the second, "He's so mental, he's irrelevant"; and of the third, "He's so spiritual, he's of no earthly good."

The Law of Balance is of course not only applicable in our personal attunement, but is also something we find acknowledged in the physical sciences, where the balancing of energy equations, chemical reactions, and mathematics is accepted procedure. We have also seen in the Laws of Begetting how the giving of actions and receiving of those same actions equalize.

Attunement involves bringing energy and pure ideas from the spiritual realm of our being into the mental/emotional and then the physical levels of expression. The balance that exists between those aspects of ourselves strongly affects that movement. One of the basic ways of working with the Law of Balance is to see that our attention is at times focused upon each of our basic natures—body, mind, heart, and spirit. Because attention directs energy, paying attention to our needs at each of these levels facilitates the movement of our vitalizing spiritual energy throughout these levels. When we fail to balance our attention, we discover the operation of the Law of Balance by our attention being brought forcefully to the neglected area of ourselves, usually through a crisis in that area of our lives. To restore healthy operation we must concentrate our attention on the neglected area until that part of our lives can again function in a healthy manner.

LEGAL CAREER IMBALANCE

I remember one of those "chance" meetings that are always very carefully set up by the Laws of Cause and Effect. It occurred at the Inn of Loretto in Santa Fe, New Mexico. About a dozen of us who had graduated from the same class in law school found ourselves comparing notes on our lives. We had been out of school for about five years and were all now successful practicing attorneys, though in many different legal fields. I was amazed to discover that more than half of us were very dissatisfied with our careers and our lives. Even though I eventually left the practice of law, I was one who was not dissatisfied. I did not understand at the time why such a large percentage of successful people were experiencing dissatisfaction. Now, as a result of having worked with many professional people and having learned of the Law of Balance, I recognize that the situation is a very normal one.

In developing a legal career or any other career, the attention is focused almost exclusively on that task. As law practice is primarily an intellectual career, the emotional and physical aspects of life, such as health, relaxation, relationships with spouses and children, get less and less attention. The spiritual needs are almost completely ignored, such as the need for time alone to contemplate, pray, and meditate. With this imbalance, the spiritual energy that keeps the different areas of our lives filled with health and vitality slows down. Our relationships suffer, our health suffers, and the satisfaction in what we have accomplished in our career isn't there. Satisfaction with the career isn't there because satisfaction is a quality of the spiritual nature, and with the neglect of the spiritual self, its vitalizing energy is diminished. The career reflects only mental energy, which is not, in the long run, vitalizing or satisfying.

The Law of Balance says that all interchanges balance. That means that if we ignore a part of our life, the law will operate to bring our attention to that part of our lives in order to balance the other investments we have made with our energy. This is not just an experience that people in mental fields have. I have known several farmers and laborers whose lives were intensely physical, but who experienced the imbalance from not spending enough time to support themselves spiritually. They also felt greatly frustrated because they did not allow themselves the time to evaluate carefully their mental and emotional decisions nor develop their capacities in those areas. Not only did their work suffer, but they began experiencing family problems and emotional depression. Their attention was drawn to their need for family time, spiritual renewal, relaxation, and in-depth mental evaluation of their activities and decisions.

Recognizing that balance requires that we focus our attention on all the various aspects of ourselves, one can legitimately ask, "How much is enough?" There are some guidelines that can serve as points of reference, but do not operate as a matter of law, because the relationship is personal and does vary for each individual. The first is the pattern acknowledged in the biblical creation story of six days of creative activity and one of rest. In terms of the giving out and renewing I have seen in people's lives over an extended period of time, the one in seven relationship appears to be helpful for many, although it is so personal it cannot be viewed as a law.

THE TITHE

The only guideline that I have seen operate on a consistent basis is the tithe. The tithe is the acknowledgment of the spiritual presence in the material realm. In Jewish law, the first tenth of everything received in the material realm was given to the spiritual work of the temple to acknowledge that God was the source of all. In this practice the acknowledgment of the spiritual presence expressing at the physical level is accomplished not only mentally, as with thoughts of thanksgiving, but also physically through the giving of the first tenth to the place where one has received spiritual nourishment. This is a powerful way of bringing the Law of Manifestation (Spirit is the life, mind is the builder, the physical is the result) and the Law of Balance into attunement with the flow of spiritual energy through the spiritual, mental, emotional, and physical levels of expression. For this reason tithing is a basic tool for achieving a life in which abundance freely expresses at the physical as well as the mental and spiritual levels of being.

I cannot present the tenth as a law in itself because some people as they began their practice of tithing have had to start with less than a tenth and yet immediately experienced the flow of attunement. Others who were advanced in their spiritual work had to go beyond the tenth to support the expansion of their awareness of the divine presence expressing in the physical realm.

The tithe is a tool for balancing attention and energy through several levels of consciousness. The conscious activity of acknowledging the spiritual source is crucial to its successful operation. Many people give regularly to spiritual work and some of those give a tenth, but if the giving is from a sense of guilt or obligation, it doesn't bring about the balance which is sought.

MICHIGAN FARM EXPERIMENT OF TITHING

While many experiences exist of individuals testing tithing as a tool for expanding their abundance, there was a very objective test that was conducted by a group of people in Michigan around 1940. They conducted their experiment in a public manner and kept careful records.

In their experiment they started with one cubic inch of wheat containing 360 kernels. They blessed the wheat and made the commitment to tithe ten percent of the harvest to their church. They then planted the wheat in a little plot behind the church.

From the first year's growth they harvested fifty cubic inches and tithed five cubic inches to the church which they fixed for the minister's breakfast. They planted the remaining nine-tenths which was forty-five cubic inches.

From the second year's growth they harvested seventy pounds of wheat. Their tithe to the church that year was seven pounds. By this time more and more people were interested in their experiment and over 350 people, including Henry Ford (who was himself a proponent of tithing), came to the dedication ceremony.

By the third year the public interest had really expanded with over 1,000 people, including the press, attending the event. The fourth year the governor of the state was in attendance, and the results were carried in the newsreels of the day. When they reached the sixth and final year of the experiment they did not have enough land to plant the wheat in. They sold the wheat to local farmers who agreed to keep careful records and to give a tenth of the harvest from the wheat to the church of their choice.

The final harvest after six years of planting nine-tenths of each year's harvest was 72,150 bushels of wheat. The tithe was 7,215 bushels.

At the start of the experiment, the people had arranged with a local miller not only to keep track of their harvest but also to compare their yields with the yield of other wheat farmers in that area. Using the state average for each year's production, the miller computed that if they had not tithed but had utilized the full ten-tenths of their crop, they would have received a yield of 5,297 bushels.

planting ten-tenths = 5,297 bushels

planting nine-tenths (one-tenth to God) = 72,150 bushels

Their tithe was greater than the entire harvest they would have received if they had not tithed.

The stunning result of this study comes not from what they did receive, but from what the miller's figures showed if they had continued to run their experiment for another six years. In the sixth year (twelfth of the experiment), there would not have been enough land mass on the planet Earth to receive the nine-tenths for another planting.

In the biblical book of Malachi, there is a promise made that if we tithed, God would " . . . pour you out a blessing that there shall not be room enough to receive it." These people showed that promise to be literally true.

This experiment demonstrates that tithing is an effective way of expanding our experience of abundance. It shows also that a different level of law must be at work in order to produce a result of such significant difference from that produced through the normal use of physical laws. The presence of the greater creative power of the spiritual at work in the physical realm is not unnatural. It is the natural result of balance between these differing creative levels being established through right use of the Universal Laws.

MENTAL/EMOTIONAL BALANCE

So far, we have looked at balance in very physical terms—the allocation of money and time. We don't really begin to discover balance until we begin to work with the balance between our head and our heart. The head controls time and resources in a constantly calculating, shifting, defining manner. I know because I used to do that. How else can you stay balanced? Set limits; know your boundaries; use time control. Well, there is another way. It is using the intelligence of the heart. In most situations, the imbalance is not what we are doing, but from where within ourselves we are doing it. Cayce pointed this out to a businessman with physical problems:

Q. Would walking through the park every morning be a means to aid this condition?

A. Provided there wasn't thinking about the man he was going to meet on the next corner or the appointment to be had at eleven or twelve o'clock . . . The physical action would be well, were . . . the companions had that would talk about

the color of the sky or the birds or the greenness of the field
or the changes of season, and not much business. This relaxation would be well but to think about other conditions
is to only make the blood run riot: "Well, I will get this over
with and do something else and get out."
Q. What will relieve the head pains?
A. Laughing will. (257-62)

At first glance this reading almost seems superficial—taking a
walk and laughing as the response to physical disease. A deeper
look brings us to present-day knowledge that most disease is
the result of our stress. In fact, seventy-five percent of all doctors' visits are for stress-related disorders. Not the stress that is
the demand of work, rather our reaction to it—our constant
worry, overanalysis, and obsession. Cayce has in fact suggested
that this man should connect with the things his heart can enjoy and release his head's preoccupation which is creating the
debilitating stress responses within his body. I once heard a very
wise teacher say that life was far too important to be taken seri-
ously. What a different response comes from the heart, which
knows solutions and sees the presence of the Creator in all
things. How appropriate to laugh at our creations. The lightest
touch of the Creator's love through our hearts uplifts and brings
solution.

For those who look at the world through their heads—one of
decisions and analysis—there is good news! Even our intellectual
endeavors can be done with heart. Then they become exciting,
renewing, and go faster as well. And Cayce's suggestion of laughter is often the best medicine for the intellectual headache.

We often try to control and balance our lives by controlling
time. As we grow in balance, the time nature of the balance equation changes dramatically. The real changes through this law
though come about when we work with mental/emotional balance. This is how we handle the thoughts in our heads and our
emotional and feeling responses to our life situations. When
these are reactive or our thoughts are churning, we are draining
our energy. We have to balance these reactions by slowing down
and spending more time on other areas of our life because oth-
erwise we do not have the energy to handle them efficiently.

Sometimes we are not reacting—most of the time we aren't.
We are just going through our day in head neutral. Instead of
angry or excited, we are in the land of indifferent—do it because

I have to. That is much better than reacting, but it is far from the feeling of quality and satisfaction we get when we connect with our hearts. We end up tired after an ordinary day. No day needs to be ordinary! It can be energizing and fun! The Law of Balance operates such that if we draw on the greater spiritual energy and intelligence available through our hearts, we get to feel and enjoy it. We give it to those around us, and it comes back to us so we get more. The more of that vitalizing spiritual energy we have, the more it balances the other aspects of our lives.

The mental/emotional imbalance happens because we are out of touch with where our guidance comes from—our hearts. From the heart we understand how to handle the things in our lives efficiently, and the energy comes to handle them quickly. As we connect with our hearts and bring balanced care into our relationships and heart intelligence into our activities, we have additional energy. Our activities become energy producing. Because we don't have to keep fixing those relationships, they give us more energy instead of taking it. We end up balancing by doing more instead of less, and we have more time for fun!

When we balance deep in our heart, we are in our "isness"— we are connected with the being we really are. Fifth-dimensional energy and intelligence can work through us so we can experience what Doc Lew Childre has called "liquid flow." Liquid flow is where a higher order of intelligence is taking us through our creation, facilitating what we are bringing forth. We are listening to our guidance and being responsive and creative. From that heart intuitive space, we hear the real needs of others and have our heart wisdom with which to respond. The project that would have taken months takes days. The difficulty we have been struggling with for a long time suddenly is amenable to a different approach and we find a solution. This happens because as we connect with our hearts we have invoked the Law of Love. The Law of Love is the ultimate balance. The love not only guides us, but that energy itself is also intelligent. Our deep heart connection produces liquid flow.

Finding our balance in the heart prevents us from having to balance by time control. It brings fun into work, the family feeling into all connections, and is the ultimate self-care. The techniques of Freeze-Frame, Cut-Thru, appreciation, care, and deep heart listening are the tools of the Law of Love and the Law of Balance. They are the connection to our higher intelligence and the doorway to grace.

I have had the privilege of teaching these tools to people in workshops all across the country. It is like giving a carpenter his first power saw or a child her first pony. Suddenly, life transforms. Not because someone tells you it will, but because you use the tool and you know life can really be different. It is just as exciting for a corporate executive as for a homemaker as for a child. When you touch the transformative power of the Law of Love, you are no longer serving time and ignorance. Greater intelligence and power are simply and easily available. You can balance your life. It happens from the balance point in you — your heart.

With balance comes the fun of life. Would you like to have more fun in your life?

Chapter 12

The Laws of One, Enlightenment, and Becoming

The light that shines above the heavens and above the world, the light that shines in the highest world, beyond which there are no others—that is the light that shines in the hearts of men.

Upanishads, Chandogya[1]

LAW OF ONE

All men will come to him who keeps to the one,
For there lie rest and happiness and peace.

Passersby may stop for music and good food.
But a description of the Tao
Seems without substance or flavor.
It cannot be seen, it cannot be heard,
And yet it cannot be exhausted.

Lao Tsu[2]

The Law of One—"God is One"

The Law of One is one of the great Laws of Attunement. This law is the first premise or principle from which all other Universal Laws spring and upon which they are based. It is the absolute basis of our lives and of creation. [3] It is called a law throughout the Cayce readings, because like a law, our relation-

ship to it determines the nature of our experience of life. However, it is not phrased as a law, and, in fact, it is not a law but
rather a Truth—a truth upon which the laws are founded and
from which they are derived. Because it is foundational to the
laws, we will speak of it as Cayce called it, "The Law of One."
This Law is so simply stated and so profound that we can easily
miss its great importance and meaning in our lives. Yet it is the
foundation principle of many of the world's great religions.

The Law of One was eventually expressed in the Jewish belief
as:

> Know, O Israel, the Lord thy God is one.

In the Muslim tradition this teaching is expressed in the
prayer:

> There is but one God, Allah . . .

In the Katha Upanishad we read:

> The Lord is One without a second. Within man He dwells
> and within all other beings. He projects the universe, main-
> tains it, and withdraws it into Himself.

To gain an insight into this law, let's look at a statement from
Cayce, where he describes our beginnings.

> . . . in the beginning . . . as He [God] moved, souls—
> portions of Himself—came into being. (263-13)

Since God is one and we as souls are each a portion of God, it
follows that the law, God is One, includes you and I as well. The
great message of the Law of One is that you and I are one with
the One. This completely contradicts the consciousness that
says that you and I are separate from the One. Since you and I
are one with the One, it follows that you and I are also one with
each other and all others. We could actually state the Law of One
as: "All are one."

ONE IN PURPOSE

How can we understand this when to our senses we are so

clearly separate? And how far does this law extend? To a man who had asked about his daily life, relationships in business, social life, and manner of worship, the reply shows there is no limit to this oneness:

> All are one, my brother. All are one; even as the Father, the Son, and the Holy Spirit are one—in purpose; but each to its own phase of experience, of manifestation; even as your body, your mind, and your soul are one. (2524-3)AR

What is the character of this Oneness? In what way can all these different forms and manifestations be one? The above reading gives the clue to one way we can experience this oneness: "in purpose." We generally consider our individual selves as one, that is, our arms, our legs, our eyes, our mind—all being parts of one. They are one in purpose—to do our will. They are all physically connected which makes the oneness easier to perceive, though the true oneness is in purpose, not in the physical connection. We can further perceive that two individuals involved in the same task, say painting a room, are one in purpose.

GARDENERS

Extending that concept further, if you and some friends are planting a garden to give all of you food for the coming year, some may be planting corn, some planting radishes, some hoeing or digging—each doing his or her own thing; yet, are you not all one in purpose, all working to the same end?

If the above analogy holds for us, the basic question is: "What is our common purpose?" The readings tell us that our purpose is to be one with the purpose of the Creative Force—God. How can we be sure what that purpose is? Well, if you wanted to join our gardening group you would come over, get acquainted, talk it over, work with us, and thereby get in tune with the group purpose. Likewise to be one with the purpose of the Creative Force, God, requires a relationship, getting acquainted, talking it over, and working together. Fortunately, there are some very simple but effective laws which explain how you can do that. The process just described is attunement—establishing a relationship, getting acquainted, learning to know each other. The greater your attunement with the One, the greater your recognition of oneness; the greater your recognition of oneness, the

greater your ability to bring forth the divine purpose for your
life.

LOVE—KEY TO ONENESS

What is the key to understanding and living the oneness? The
following reading brings us back again to love:

> For, ever has been, ever will be, the law of One the same.
> "Love in your daily experience. Apply in your daily activities
> the love that you would have the Father show you, in your
> relationships to your fellows, do [if you] know the Law of
> One." (497-1)AR

And what kind of love would you like to have others show
you? Would it not be wonderful if others loved you exactly as you
are, without any reservations, any requirements that you should
do this or that or be different in any way; in other words, without judgments of any sort. That would truly be unconditional
love, loving you not in spite of conditions, but loving you for
what you are. It is this unconditional love with which you need
to love yourself and to love others if you would live in accord
with the Law of One.

EXPERIENCES OF ONENESS

To fully grasp the complete and profound significance of the
Law of One is an ever-expanding exploration for human consciousness. It may well always be for us an ultimate which we
seek to understand and discover in ever-increasing increments
of intelligence.

There are many people who have had experiences of this oneness at a profound personal level. For a time at least, they have
broken through or moved into an awareness of oneness and have
then attempted to share the experience, although they all seem
to agree it is beyond description. These experiences are not
something to seek. The persons to whom they came did not seek
them out, and the teaching and laws point us toward living more
effective lives in the earth, rather than reaching for cosmic experiences. However, these experiences give us a glimpse into the
greater reality of which we are very much a part. They may be
helpful in dropping many of the concepts of separation with

which we have viewed ourselves and others.

When Bruce and I began to work with or study a law, there always came to us examples or opportunities to help us better understand that truth. Such was the case with the Law of One. At a week-long conference at A.R.E. headquarters in 1980, we were both presenting our understandings of the laws. Bruce presented the Law of One to that conference. Afterward a young man came to him and told him this experience. In a previous year this young man's life seemed to be without meaning when one day he was amazed to find that whenever he looked at another person he saw his own face. No matter who it was or what that person was doing or how many there were, each person he saw had his own face. This went on for days and he came to realize in this dramatic fashion that we are all one. The experience completely changed his life for it brought a whole new view of life and understanding of its meaning for him.

Many years ago, in 1901, a Canadian doctor, Richard M. Bucke, M.D., published a study which has become a classic. It describes people's experience of the onenes or, as he termed it, cosmic consciousness. He relates more than fifty cases and comments on the characteristics of this experience:

> The prime characteristic of cosmic consciousness is, as its name implies, a consciousness of the cosmos, that is, of the life and order of the universe. Along with the consciousness of the cosmos there occurs an intellectual enlightenment or illumination which alone would place the individual on a new plane of existence—would make him almost a member of a new species. To this is added a state of moral exaltation, an indescribable feeling of elevation, elation, and joyousness, a quickening of the moral sense, which is fully as striking and more important both to the individual and to the race than is the enhanced intellectual power. With these come, what may be called a sense of immortality, a consciousness of eternal life, not a conviction that he shall have this, but the consciousness that he has it already.[4]

It was not long after the appearance of the first articles that Bruce had written on Universal Law that he received a letter from a lady who mentioned she had experienced oneness. He wrote asking her to tell him about it. This is her reply telling of her wonderful experience:

First I would like to mention that as a teenager my religious mother had told me that sometimes during a special event in one's life one might receive a "blessing." I had hoped that such a "blessing" might come to me, but I supposed I probably wasn't "good enough." The point I'm trying to make is that, other than my belief in a blessing, when I did have a spiritual experience, it came with no effort on my part. I did not pray for it, nor meditate, nor in any way try to make it happen—it just came. And what also amazes me is the fact that I was young, twenty years old and a very ordinary person.

The entire experience actually covered a period of four or five months. It began with a feeling of not being afraid—so much so that I was puzzled, and I told myself that I must face facts and realize there are things to fear—but even so I still felt unafraid. As time went on this developed into a wonderful state of tranquility, but not just being quiet and restful, but a rather dynamic sort of tranquility in which there was no fear, no tension, no nervousness. This culminated in the most wonderful thing that ever happened to me and the most happiness I have ever known.

I was at one (at-one-ment) with every other living person on earth. I did not seem to lose my identity, but yet there was no separateness, all was one. I knew that the God in me was the same God that was in everyone else—making us all one—so there could be no separateness. There was only the one in the entire world, and this oneness filled all space. It was not a vision. I did not see anything, except that I seemed to see the figure filling all space. And yet I felt it, I lived it, I knew it. It was so real, more real than so-called real life. It is hard to put it into words because the feeling of happiness was so great, and the total absence of all fear and the wonderful feeling of safety (safe in the arms of Jesus, as the song goes) and "in Him we live and move and have our being." It was a tremendous experience.

I had not read about the oneness before my experience, had never even heard of it. I feel I have not expressed it adequately—words can't seem to convey the whole wonder of it.

These two experiences and the many cases cited by Dr. Bucke show the possibility of a reality beyond the one of separateness we normally hold. This reality is set forth or defined by the Truth of One. The reality is that we are all one.

THE LAW OF ENLIGHTENMENT

The light of the body is the eye: if therefore thine eye be single, thy whole body shall be full of light. Matthew 6:22 (KJV)

The Law of Enlightenment—"When one sees only God, the whole being is filled with light."

Through the Law of Enlightenment, we bring the powerful truth of the Law of One into application in our lives. In its simplest form, this law says that everything in life is the Divine expressing, and when one can see life with that perception, an experience of being filled with light takes place—enlightenment. Being filled with light is the experience of feeling peace and love. God is absolute goodness. To live in the application of this law is to experience that absolute goodness in one's life.

The challenge of comprehending the perception of the "One," the divine presence, that activates this law in a person's life is that the world appears to our ordinary perception to be tremendously dualistic. We see all around us health and disease, joy and pain, plenty and poverty, war and peace, justice and injustice, wisdom and ignorance.

When one first begins to attempt to apply this law, there is an intermediate stage of application in which one discovers that the goodness of God can be found in the midst of even the greatest pain. We say God's good is in the midst of it, but we cannot yet say there is only God's goodness. There is still the acknowledgment of the apparent evil as being real, but it is unable to obscure the experience of the divine presence or the light for that individual. Wholeness and peace are experienced by that person in the midst of the negativity. Remember that the laws operate in ratios. It is to the extent that the conditions of the law are applied that the results are produced by the law. This is an example of seeing in part the oneness of God in the situation. So the enlightenment brings the new perception to mind to a degree and the person feels some peace—some presence of God's love at work.

Because this is only a partial application of the law, there are
other steps that can be taken as one approaches the full application of the law.

> Know first and foremost, as has been given, that the Lord
> your God is *one!* Then know, too, that you are one—your
> ego, your I Am. Your purposes, then; your heart and your
> life must be a *consistent* thing!
> For if your eye be single . . . then your *whole body* is full
> of light. (1537-1)AR

The above reading encourages us to focus on our purpose and
live in our hearts with consistency. This is a part of our bringing
about a fuller relationship to this law in our lives. As our ratio of
seeing God in our lives grows, everything in life, including that
which we judge as wrong, bad, or evil is perceived as that same
divine goodness. The experience itself is difficult to put into
words, yet the perception in application is to some degree ex-
plainable.

It is as though we experience ourselves growing. The Universal Laws let us meet our creations that express less than the
total love of which they are capable. They may be creations that
are outwardly painful, but the deeper experience is of the presence of love teaching, uplifting, and freeing. There is only God.
The creation is but a form we put on the Divine. When we relate
to the presence instead of the form, there is only the absolute
goodness that is the presence of God.

SNOW SCULPTURES

If you were asked to look upon a field of snow sculptures,
some would appear to be of monsters or of war, expressing the
negative expressions of life. Some sculptures would be of beautiful things, of exciting scenes and of royal balls. There would be
those covered in dirt, some would be as hard ice, and others
would be softest snow. As you looked at the sculptures, you realized that you were the one who made each sculpture. On one
you learned about ice, on another you learned to express joy, on
another you learned to express fear, on another hate, another
peace, another softness. In some of the sculptures you were in
touch with the order and beauty that is inherent in the snow. In
other sculptures, you experienced and expressed in the form of

your sculpture what it was like to have lost touch with the order, majesty, and beauty of the snow. Yet with each work the very laws that directed your actions and experiences of the snow taught you of the choices that you had as a sculptor and of the differing experiences that you brought forth as you exercised those choices.

As you reviewed your sculptures of snow, you found your perception changing again into expanded insight. You remembered experiencing a love that radiated to you from within each flake of snow and supported you in all your learning and creating. At every step it said to you, "Understand this creation of joy; understand this creation of fear." Yet it never judged your creation. It always opened to you the understanding of yourself as a creator. As you looked at each sculpture, what you saw was not the form you put the snow in, but the beauty of the snow. Your eyes no longer dwelt on the form, but gazed directly at the perfect order, beauty, and sparkling energy that was in each snowflake regardless of the form you had molded it into. You realized the greatest thing you gained was not the forms or the learning, but the ability to relate to the perfection of the snow itself. Each sculpture you now saw was that crystalline presence, the beauty that was perfect in sculptured form and remained perfect after the form was gone and only the perfect presence of snow remained.

The snow analogy shares a spirit of the vision of which this law speaks even though it falls far short of representing the true relationship with the Divine. Part of the difficulty in understanding this law is that it involves a capability to see beyond both appearances and paradox.

FILLED WITH LIGHT

What is the experience of being "filled with light" that is promised by this law? We have probably all experienced it in some degree, because we have all reached for the highest within ourselves in response to both difficult and very pleasant experiences. There have been times for all of us when we have broken through our patterns of judgment and simply perceived the expression of the Divine in the simple forms of our everyday lives.

Remember the experience of watching your children at play, taking delight, not in whether they were doing something right or wrong, but in the sheer beauty and vitality of the life force that animated those marvelous beings. That sense of wonder and joy you felt was the light. Remember looking at someone you loved—each may have been doing the simplest of tasks, or even sleeping—but you allowed yourself to completely love and accept each just as he or she was that moment—no judgment—just a sense of warmth and delight touching your heart. That was the experience of the light.

The difficulty with the language of this law is that when we hear, "filled with light," we tend to think of scenes like Moses receiving the tablets in the midst of swirling nonearthly forces in Cecil B. DeMille's movie, *The Ten Commandments*. We conceptualize extraordinary experiences that have nothing to do with the lives we live. This law operates for everyone, everyday. Occasionally we may hear of extraordinary experiences, and someone will write a book about it. However, the beauty of this law is that it fills the ordinary with beauty, the day-to-day with the warmth and meaning that brings "down home" satisfaction to life.

Remember when you were in the midst of a crisis and suddenly you stopped for a moment and laughed at yourself for all the seriousness and all the worry. You knew that you were merely experiencing life and that even at that moment you could touch the goodness. Your laughter was the gift of the light, an illumined or expanded perception of your life.

Often I have heard people who work with Hospice, the organization that gives support to individuals and families facing terminal illnesses, describe the experience of finding great peace for themselves and for those with whom they were working when they suddenly saw the beauty of what seemed a difficult and tragic process on the outside—families relating and supporting each other, people finding a resolution of questions within themselves, and suddenly experiencing moments of love and growing together. That discovery was the experience of the light—enlightenment or illumination of the greater truth within the experience.

Notice how each of the examples has an expression of love at the core. When we truly align with the One, we are love expressing. The divine presence is love, and it is flowing through us. The gift from the love is light. So as we love, we are filled with light—enlightened.

There are also the experiences of the mystics and the seekers from all ages who have had great, powerful, and transforming experiences with what they have called the light. These too are available to all of us through this Law of Enlightenment. However, the law is not just for mystics. In the daily moments when we allow ourselves to see the one presence that is the only true reality of life, we experience the fulfillment of this most beautiful of spiritual laws.

Perhaps you have heard of someone who has gone through the experience of "enlightenment" or is an enlightened being. Such concepts of enlightenment seem so far away for us ordinary people who are still trying to put food on the table, get the kids to school on time, and keep the car running. The Law of Enlightenment works for all of us. It is an experience of ratios, just as all the laws are. You may be talking to a friend about a challenge and see your friend as growing in courage. That is seeing the presence of God in your friend. To the extent that you experienced that presence, you are filled with light. Maybe it happens a little more next week. In six months, it may be a frequent occurrence. The law assures us that every step we make, there will be the response of that inner light and love to our being.

INVOKING THE LAW

How do we invoke the Law of Enlightenment? How, when we are in the midst of life's stresses that seem so dualistic, do we connect with our ability to perceive the presence of God there at work in our lives, unfolding itself through our experiences? How do we make that shift in perception? The answer is very simple. Go to your heart!

In chapter 3 (fig. 3C), we saw the beautiful, harmonious order of the coherent heart frequencies that are generated when your core heart feelings stimulate the neurocortex of the brain. This, with the electromagnetic signal from your heart, supports a shift in perception guided by the intelligence of your heart. Your heart intelligence has the capacity to bring the perception and understanding of the divine presence into your experience—to open your higher vision to "see only God." Through the Law of Enlightenment, you are filled with the light—the light of understanding, the light of joy, the light of peace. What a beautiful world you behold! You see heaven on earth!

HEAVEN ON EARTH

Well, how did you think it was going to get here? Clouds floating along the ground? That is fog. Golden streets? That is an
inefficient use of natural resources. Heaven is perception. When
you see God everywhere, when you experience God in everything
you do, you are in the kingdom of God. You are in heaven with
God right here on earth. Heaven on earth is a frequency given by
the Creator as we express His higher purpose and power through
His laws. The access code to those frequencies—the key to those
laws —is the love in your heart.

The Law of Becoming—"As you live the law, you become the law."

Even at the level of our society's functioning, this law becomes
apparent. We have seen time and again where people have
worked so diligently with the expression of a principle that they
become inseparable from that principle. Dr. Martin Luther King,
Jr., with civil rights, George Washington and Thomas Jefferson
with the founding of the United States, or Dr. Sigmund Freud
with psychoanalysis.

When we look at civil rights, we must deal with the concepts
that Dr. King brought into expression, the progress that he
helped the nation make, and the dream he held before us. Today
we experience part of the creation his efforts helped bring about.
When we exercise the powers of government or examine those
powers, we must deal with that which was expressed through
Washington, who led the fight for freedom and established the
model for the presidency, and Jefferson's ideas of what this
country idealized in the Declaration of Independence. When we
work with introspection or seek assistance from a psychothera-
pist, the basic concepts we are involved with are there in society's
awareness and our awareness through association with Dr.
Sigmund Freud.

These people gave such expression to the principles that they
developed that, even though they all left their bodies years ago,
we work with their ideas, continuing to define and develop them.

There is an even clearer experience of becoming the law as
one works with the spiritual levels of expression. We become
that which we express. If we choose to express love, we become
the expression of that love in that minute, in that place, and

situation. The same is true if we seek to express anger, power, joy, or peace.

> Through that love, as man makes it manifest in his own heart and life, does it reach that law, and in compliance of a law, the law becomes *a* part of the individual. (3744-5)

To understand the fullness of this law, remember when someone expressed to you total unconditional love. That person became at that moment the presence of love in your world. By the Law of Attraction, his or her expression of love called forth the response of love, that which was the divine presence within you. The Law of Love was activated within you because that person was love. What was the difference between that person's love, the presence of God, and your own power of love? There was no line of distinction unless we choose to draw one. God—Love—is One.

> For the law was given by Moses, but grace and truth came by Jesus Christ. John 1:17 (KJV)

Once we understand the universal laws, the meaning of this statement in the opening chapter of John is clear. The law Moses taught was the Law of Cause and Effect. In order to help the people of Israel free themselves of pain and suffering through these laws, Moses gave the Ten Commandments, which became the basis of the social and religious laws of Judaism. Jesus not only taught the Law of Grace and the Law of Truth, but He lived them so completely that He became one with their expression in the Earth. Thus millions of people have been able to relate to and demonstrate these laws through their relationship with Him. He literally became the expression of the Laws of Grace and Truth.

Yet these laws are universal and not the property of Christianity or any religious movement or teaching. They have also been demonstrated and taught by all the great religious teachers of the world, and by all who loved and by all who sought the truth of the divine presence.

PATRICK'S GRANDMOTHER

Patrick was a man in his forties who had faced and overcome

many challenges in his life but who still found himself constantly doubting his own value and his own capability. In exploring these feelings, his memory showed him an experience from his childhood where he was severely punished and criticized by his father, whose approval he tried so hard to get, yet never received. As he sought to heal those feelings, he tried to reach out to that frightened, hurt, little boy within him, but he found he couldn't bring himself to love him. He knew how much that hurt, immature part of himself had expressed itself in his life at the times when he needed maturity, creativity, and sound judgment. The result was always wrong decisions and failure. He saw that part of himself as weak, wrong, and unacceptable.

Patrick tried to ask Jesus for that love, but Jesus had become for him a figure like his father who judged him when he made mistakes, so he could not feel any love there. Patrick did remember that there was one person who had always loved him. That was his grandmother. It didn't matter what he had done, she was always glad to see him and to put her arms around him and understand. As he brought her memory to mind, he could feel her willingness to reach out to this frightened child within him and enfold him in her love. She held that little boy in Patrick's mind while the tears came and the power of that divine presence touched those deep places of hurt and brought healing and peace. The love of that grandmother was the presence that brought healing for Patrick and began to free him from the limiting self-perceptions that had manifested in his life for so long. She was the love that allowed Patrick to reconnect with his own heart. The hurts were healed, and Patrick's life began to reflect the confidence and creativity that expressed his long-suppressed abilities.

That grandmother lived the Law of Love. She accepted that little boy unconditionally, expressing her love to him. Years after her passing from the earth she was the expression of the presence of love in the earth for Patrick. She became the Law of Love, a timeless healing presence, the expression of the Divine. As you live the law, you become the law.

Chapter 13

Grace

All this universe is in the glory of God, of Siva the god of love. The heads and faces of men are his own and he is in the hearts of all.

He is indeed the Lord supreme whose grace moves the hearts of men. He leads us unto his own joy and to the glory of his light.

Svetasvatara Upanishad

Then, as you grow in grace, using that you know to do, there is given strength, hope, and peace. Such peace as the world, or the rabble, knoweth not, but that which even in the face of seeming disaster makes it possible that through tears there may come the shining light of His love, that you may pass on to those that you meet—yes, in the street, in the home, in the quietness of thine meditations, in the throng; and that every thought, every act, becomes a *song* in the heart and a joy in the service of being not just good but good in His name! (272-7)AR

WHAT IS GRACE?

The subject of grace is a mystery to most, is misunderstood by many, and is wrapped in veils of illusion for all of us. However, through study of the Cayce readings one can come to appreciate a portion of the meaning and significance of grace. I have learned that the description given by the song, "Amazing Grace," is no exaggeration. The grace of God is the catalyst that makes our life and growth in the earth possible, and it works for us constantly. The readings affirm that where we are in the world, the condition or position we are in, our race, our color, the fact that we are even here and alive, all that we have, all that we see, all that happens to us — all are dependent on and a result of the grace of God.

We experience grace as the movement of God's love. It occurs in our lives so frequently in everyday life that people do not recognize that it is the same thing that is involved in what appears to be a miraculous experience. We feel its effects in simple ways such as the upliftment of our thoughts and feelings. Remember when you were worried about a situation and suddenly you let yourself drop that worry and had a feeling of well-being, of hope, or of a right outcome being possible? That was the experience of grace. It's as simple as experiencing the beauty in sunlight dancing on leaves and the sense of serenity in the fall of snow. It's as startling as the miraculous healing of disease and the birth of a child. Its effects are seen in the solution to world problems and in our growing understandings of other people. Its power is unlimited.

While grace (the movement of that which is the Divine) is always taking place, we only consciously experience that movement and its true nature when we open ourselves to it. Our whole experience of creating is the expression of grace, because the spiritual presence moving from the spiritual level of our being through the mental to the physical is what we utilize to make our creation. However, most of the time our attention is on the limited nature of our creation or caught up in a mental, emotional, or physical response to it. We experience the presence of grace when our awareness is open to its nature. Sometimes that is by intentionally opening our awareness. At other times we are awakened to it by events such as an unexpected healing, appreciating the beauty in nature, the end of a war, or the birth of a child.

Grace is not a law, but it is a supporting structure on which our lives are built. It is always there for us. We would not exist without it. It is there for all, both criminals and saints, without distinction. It is not something you have to work for or that you can start or even stop. Divine grace, like God, simply is.

For His grace is sufficient unto the end. He that endureth the cross shall wear the crown; not he that gives up, that cries "Enough" and is ready to quit, but they that press on even when there apparently is no way out. (303-6)

This reading is telling us God's grace is always sufficient. Things are never hopeless, no condition is ever really incurable, there is always a way out, and all things are possible through grace. With this in mind, the readings also refer to grace as God's rain check! In other words, no matter how discouraging, how difficult, or how impossible things seem, there is grace, good, in the midst of it hidden only by the clouds of our misunderstandings. The day is coming when the sun will shine for you, and you can see and feel and enjoy the beauty of the universe and find meaning and good in your life. Grace is God's rain check! [1]

SUN ANALOGY

A physical analogy for our experience of grace is our experience of the sun. The radiance of the sun is the physical source of our life experience just as the flow of God's love is the source of our life. The radiance of the sun is necessary to our existence and all that is available to us in the earth environment. Everything we experience here is dependent on the sun that allows us to have this life form and that permits the life processes we use in all our interactions. Every physical thing we interact with is the result of the sun, whether it is made of trees that the sun gave life to or the chemicals and minerals that were formed through our planet's evolution as a part of our solar system. Yet the sun does not say how we must use that to which it has given life.

In our analogy, the movement of the Divine is the animating force of our lives as the sun's radiance is at the physical level. It is that which gives us consciousness and vitalizes our mental and emotional being. At the physical level, that love is also the divine presence which brings our creations into manifestation in the physical world. It does not tell us how to utilize that which it provides. Yet unlike the sun, that divine presence has its own intelligence that we can turn to in discovering our highest relationship to its life expressions.

As with the Divine, we are not always aware of the sun and its effects on our lives. It can appear to be something quite removed from the earth and our experience, or something that has a very limited role such as thinking of the sun as only the heat and light we feel. It can even appear that the sun is at times not present simply because at night we are unable to see it directly. We can hold the same perception of the expression of the Divine. It can seem remote, not having a direct influence on us or altogether absent because we are not able to perceive it directly. Yet even in the night of our ignorance, it is that presence that is sustaining our life while we learn of its omnipresence and our true relationship to it.

GRACE AND THE LAWS

The Universal Laws are Laws of Grace. They are a part of the grace of God that is designed to bring us to greater understanding of God and to know ourselves as one with God. Spirit's purpose is to help us achieve that; therefore, the purpose of grace is to give us everything we need to raise our consciousness to the point of recognizing our oneness with God. That includes all the talent, all the ability, all the power we need in order to raise our consciousness. Plus we are given the free will to use that power and guidance as we choose.

Through the laws we utilize all this to cocreate our reality—to experience our creation. It is up to us to decide how to use it. Chaos, misery, trauma, war, and suffering occur for us as individuals and as nations when we misuse the power and misapply the Universal Laws we have been given through grace. We often misuse them unintentionally when we rely on our own mental powers and forget the most important aspect of grace—God's guidance. We end up creating our difficulties, problems, chaos, and trauma. The laws give us the opportunity to learn our lessons and gradually wake up to who we really are and can be. Eventually we learn that we can get all the guidance we need and use it in ways that will bring joy, peace, and happiness to ourselves and others.

SPONTANEOUS GRACE

Lynn Sparrow in her book, *Reincarnation: Claiming Your Past, Creating Your Future*, beautifully describes the spontaneity of grace.

The direct awareness of grace—what I have called appre-
hending it—sometimes comes upon us spontaneously, like
a happy surprise or realization . . . One Cayce reading aptly
describes this spontaneous awareness of grace as a sudden
experience of "harmony and beauty and grace" that causes
us to wonder what moved us to feel different in that moment (no. 3098-2). We may experience such a moment on a
spring morning, when the new life all around us affirms
that life is good after all; or on a cold winter evening, when
home is warm and cozy. These are the moments that go
beyond happiness or pleasure or even contentment; they
are brief moments when the external and internal worlds
meet in harmony, and we catch a glimpse of the ultimate
goodness of life; and they are reminders to us that we are a
part of that harmony. In such moments we experience
grace, even if we cannot define it.[2]

The Law of Fulfillment—"Love fulfills the law."

Teacher, which is the great commandment in the law?
And he [Jesus] said to him, "You shall love . . . And a
second is like it, You shall love . . . On these two commandments depend all the law . . . "

Jesus   (Matthew 22:36 RSV)

" . . . love is the fulfilling of the law."

Apostle Paul (Romans 13:10 RSV)

Part of the secret to understanding the Laws of Transformation is that they do not contradict the Laws of Cause and Effect,
nor set aside their operation. The Laws of Transformation fulfill
the purpose of the Laws of Cause and Effect. This is because
they are a part of the Law of Fulfillment and the experience of
grace that is expressed through this law. The Law of Fulfillment
is "Love fulfills the law." This is not the totality of grace, because
grace is much more than one law. All the laws are an expression
of grace. However, this one law expresses the state of grace so
clearly that it could be called a Law of Grace.

JIM AND SHEILA

Even though the Law of Fulfillment is very broad and powerful, we often experience it working in the simplest of ways. Jim and Sheila experienced the Law of Fulfillment in a very painful moment of their life. Jim came in late from work very tired, both from physical exhaustion and from dealing with the unresponsiveness of the people with whom he worked. Sheila, who was worn out from the demands of the children and a new baby, was irritated over the wasted efforts of fixing a nice dinner that the family hadn't eaten together. Their feelings at first came out in the tenseness of the silence until the children were finally asleep. Then they surfaced as the argument.

Each became more and more accusing and the hurt and anger grew until suddenly in the midst of his anger Jim saw what was really hurting him. Nothing they were arguing about hurt as much as hurting this person he loved. He told Sheila that. He told her that he did love her and that he was sorry. As he ceased his attacks and acknowledged his love, she was able to also. The love they allowed themselves to feel healed the pain of the angry words. Instead of blaming each other, they experienced the support and help each needed from the other. They had started to create resentment, blame, and separation in their marriage. As they felt their love and concern for each other, the limited creation they had begun was released.

FULFILLING THE LAW

The only purpose of that limited creation would have been to allow them to experience what their harsh words had created in their marriage so that they could develop their ability to create with greater wisdom. Having made the choice to express the highest, their love fulfilled the law. The release from the angry emotions, the closeness they felt, and the renewal of their support for each other was the experience of grace.

The best understanding of the Law of Fulfillment was shared with humankind through the image and example of Jesus working with the law. Jesus explained His function as one who would embody love and thus give expression to grace operating through the Law of Fulfillment in this way: "I came not to abolish the law and the prophets, but to fulfill them." (Matthew 5:17 RSV)

One of the purposes of the Laws of Cause and Effect is to allow us, as cocreators with the Divine, to fully experience our own creations. In this way we learn what our thoughts and actions have created, and we develop our ability to bring forth creations which manifest the wholeness, love, and wisdom that we are capable of through our spiritual nature. We learn this step by step as we live through what we have created. As we learn to respond to life situations with the wisdom of our hearts, we are able to give ever fuller expression to the love that indwells us. Love is the expression of our spiritual nature.

Love fulfills the law. At the point in our development when we are giving full expression to the love that indwells us, there is no further need to work with that old creation for two reasons. First, we have accomplished the purpose for its existence, which is to teach us to live the love that is the expression of our true nature. Secondly, we have met enough of our old creation with love that it has been transformed. In meeting the old situation with love, we are living according to the Law of Fulfillment. Our love has fulfilled the purpose of the Laws of Cause and Effect. The Law of Fulfillment results in freeing us from the limiting nature of the old creation. Having learned what that lesson was about, we graduate from that class.

Is there a Law of Grace? Cayce gave more than 14,000 readings and mentioned grace in over 300 of them. However nowhere in there does he give a Law of Grace. Grace is too broad to be contained within one definition of its operation. The Law of Fulfillment gives expression to our experience of grace by which the loving presence of God frees us from one level of experience and lifts us to another. Every time we take a step in the direction of a higher response to life, the operation of grace is involved, making gentler that process. The dishonest person who takes the step toward honesty finds grace facilitating that step, gentling that which the cause-and-effect laws return to him or her. Each step builds until in a consciousness of love we see the purpose of the law fulfilled.

The passkeys to that wonderful world of grace are the Universal Laws. The Law of Fulfillment is one of its most important keys. This is the law we must come to know and live if we are going to graduate from this school of law and make our transformation to that world of grace. It is by learning and living this law that we can really come to apprehend the grace that exists in our life and create it for others.

The significance of the Law of Fulfillment is tremendous. *The whole purpose of the Universal Laws is to help you grow in grace, knowledge, and understanding so that you may, as Christ did, overcome the world. This means you can overcome your trials,* tribulations, troubles, and sorrows no matter what they may be and move to a state of grace, of peace, joy, and happiness. This is true transformation. The Law of Fulfillment gives you the one single, simple key to achieving that heaven on earth. It gives the key to the whole shebang, not just to one little problem or to a big problem but the key to all problems. Most important of all, you can make it from karma to grace by Universal Law! And you know that means it is immutable, unchangeable, and works for everyone, everywhere all the time! There are no ifs, ands, buts, or maybes about Universal Law. It works always. All you have to do is apply it.

GROWING IN GRACE

To effectively apply this law we need to know how to do it. The readings term this process growing in grace. This is Bruce's description of one such experience.

I can assure you that this process for moving from karma to grace works. Many years ago I faced the toughest karmic situation of my life. I had an excellent job as one of the top executives in a corporation, and a wonderful family. I should have been extremely happy, but wasn't. My boss at that time was a very astute businessman with whom I had to work closely. We could always agree on what should be done, but I found myself continually at odds with him on how it should be done and became increasingly critical of him and his way of running the company. It was truly a karmic situation, though I didn't even know what that meant at that time until I learned of Edgar Cayce and began to attend an Edgar Cayce study group.

Gradually I came to realize that I was involved in a karmic situation, that I was responsible for it, that what I disliked in my boss was a reflection of my own faults, and that I had some lessons to learn. It took me quite a few years to come to fully accept and understand all this for I had to make a major shift in my consciousness. But as I did come to understand and to accept that I was responsible for the situation, I was able to stop blaming him, to see the lesson it had for me, to become thankful for the condition, and to realize that my boss was providing me with a wonderful opportunity for better knowing myself and for my growth.

I began to drop my criticism and complaints and even to appreciate his many wonderful qualities and abilities. It was not long after this shift in my consciousness occurred that conditions became such that I could retire long before the normal retirement age to a beautiful place in the mountains, truly a move from karma to grace.

BECOMING AWARE OF GRACE

Many times grace is presented as something amazing or mysterious that happens or occurs without rhyme or reason and may happen to anyone without distinction. While that is true to a degree, it is only one aspect of grace. In addition, the readings convey another very important and more complete and realistic picture. They portray grace as an important part of our lives which we can both develop and apply. Not only that, but they show us how we can be subject to or receive grace—not indiscriminately, but in accord with Universal Laws.

How may we become aware of grace? The answer is by living a life that is based on the spiritual. This means our desires and hopes are not for fortune, position, or power, but our hopes and desires are to manifest and glorify Spirit, to bring greater love and care into the world, and to deepen the spiritual connection in our lives. With that as our basis as we then apply the Universal Laws in the highest ways—in particular the Golden Rule—we grow in our awareness of the abiding grace, that grace that is always with us.

THANK YOU, FATHER

Let me share with you a simple but highly effective way you can open yourself to the awareness of grace. Everett Irion, a highly respected writer and teacher of the Cayce readings, found one of the better ways for dealing with our karmic situations, a way that in my experience and in that of many others is very effective. Regardless of the kind of situation in which you find yourself, he advocates that you face it by saying and truly meaning, "Thank you, Father." You are thanking the Father for this situation and for the lesson it has for you.

EXAMPLES

Shirley was having a great deal of difficulty with a fellow employee. She had heard of the "Thank you, Father" approach and finally in desperation one weekend decided to try it. Through prayer and recognition of the fact that she had drawn the situation to herself, she was finally able to accept it with love. She was then able to say and mean, "Thank you, Father." Shortly after she arrived at work on Monday, a supervisor approached Shirley and offered her the opportunity to transfer to another department!

By this simple act of bringing herself more in accord with and finding the love in the situation, Shirley had fulfilled the law. She thereby dealt with the karma involved so the need for this situation in her life had ended. She had changed her consciousness and entered a new hologram; therefore, her outer situation changed accordingly.

In another case, a girl had recently come to Virginia Beach and attended a lecture by Everett Irion. Some weeks later she awoke one morning with a terribly painful crick in her neck. She had no money, but decided she had to go to the doctor. Before leaving, she thought of "Thank you, Father" and began to use it in order to accept her painful situation with love and thankfulness. Holding her head in her hands to ease the pain, she went out the door. As she did so the door slammed, striking her elbow and jarring her neck back into place! Mere coincidence? There is another Universal Law that goes: "Nothing happens by chance."

A letter to the A.R.E. newsletter revealed another case. A couple who were employed by the State Department wrote telling of their experience. They had been assigned to go to some primitive outpost which they felt was the last place they would have chosen. However, they worked diligently to accept the situation and to see the good in it, to truly be able to sincerely say, "Thank you, Father." Just a short while before they were due to leave, their orders were canceled, and they were reassigned to the place where they really wanted to go! That is moving from karma to grace!

What actually is happening in the use of the simple phrase, "Thank you, Father," is that you are bringing yourself to look at the situation from a higher point of view, to see the good (love of the Father) in the situation. Thus as you bring love to the situation, you are applying the Law of Fulfillment: **Love fulfills the**

law. It does indeed and so the situation is resolved. As it is re-solved, you become aware of the grace that results from the action of love in your life.

"Thank you, Father" is not a mere technique. When used sincerely it is a real recognition not only of the Law of Fulfillment but also of the karmic laws, the Laws of Cause and Effect involved in our situations. It will work if you truly come to recognize and accept that you are the cause of all that happens to you, that the Father, through His infinite love for you, has provided these laws for your benefit and opportunity for growth, and that all that happens to you, no matter how painful or disturbing it may be, is an opportunity for you to grow and is what you need at this time. Sincerely going to your heart, you can say and truly mean, "Thank you, Father." At that point you no longer need that situation; you are no longer trying to deal with it on a karmic level; you have accepted it and risen above it; you have brought love to it and fulfilled the law—you have moved from karma to grace! You then become aware of the grace.

DIMENSIONS OF GRACE

We experience grace in different ways depending upon the dimensional energy with which we are working. In the third dimension, one of the expressions of grace is that we get to experience one event at a time. The gift of time enables us to work sequentially so we are not overwhelmed by the press of events as we experience our creation. Grace often seems to slow down events while we work them out. As we approach the fifth-dimensional energy, grace operates to speed the events up. The expression of grace at that dimension is that it efficiently transforms, instead of processes, what is not supportive to divine purpose. This energy from the higher fourth and fifth dimensions makes it clear when we are out of harmony with the purpose of the laws. When we do not listen to our guidance or are out of integrity with ourselves, it feeds back quickly on our systems so we learn faster and do not have to spend long times in a disharmonious state.

The speedup we are experiencing in our world at this time is a part of grace. It is the divine higher-dimensional energy entering the earth system bringing higher intelligence closer to our hearts and releasing the density of our past thoughts and creations. In its love, it is asking you to awaken to who you are, to connect with your love and care so that you are in tune with life. It is offering you higher intelligence solutions to your problems. But as with all of grace, it is your choice to be aware of it or not—to turn to your heart or stay in your old mind-sets. The wonderful gift of this grace is that the tremendous love and care of God is there, ready to guide you, embrace you, and lift you up as you open your heart to amazing grace.

Conclusion

The Laws of Cause and Effect are the forces with which we create the experiences of our lives most moments of the day. Our thoughts and feelings, beliefs, actions, and choices create most of our experiences. With God's freely given energy, through His laws, we are the creators of our lives. These laws give us the opportunity to experience and understand ourselves as creative beings and the results of our creations. They give us the gift of being able to take responsibility for our lives. The laws are the expression of a tremendous order and love. Yet in our immaturity we often use them to create painful experiences and continue the creation of very limiting patterns. Fortunately, there is a constant opportunity to create something higher, filled with the promise of meaning and fulfillment.

To free ourselves from the limiting patterns that we have created, we turn to the Laws of Transformation. We fulfill the purpose of the Laws of Cause and Effect when we bring into our experience the expression of love. As we love, the Law of Love transforms our old patterns. Through laws such as the Law of Faith, we are able to bring into expression the divine blueprint which is encoded upon our hearts. The Laws of Transformation are the instruments through which we bring the goodness and intelligence of God into expression in our lives.

Bringing these powerful laws into our lives is not difficult. There are tools and techniques—Freeze-Frame, Cut-Thru, prayer, meditation, care, and appreciation—that even our scientific world is discovering give expression to these greater levels of intelligence and order. They are simple yet powerful keys to unlocking the doorway to the infinite, through the love in our hearts.

As we experience our new creation of wholeness, we seek for some way not to fall back into the old patterns of creating the limited experiences of our past. For this we are provided with the Laws of Attunement.

Our experiences with the Laws of Attunement are as diverse as the mundane, outer-oriented questions about the price of a house and as powerful and profound as the awareness of who we truly are and the understanding of what we are doing here on planet Earth. As we turn to our hearts and ask, the divine intelligence and guidance is there responding to us. We are constantly shown the path of transformation. As we choose love's response, we grow in our ability to manifest the highest within us. As we live in accordance with these laws, we begin to walk the earth, aware of the amazing grace that is constantly, moment by moment lifting us higher, bringing the higher dimensions of the divine pattern into expression in our world. Through the deep love in our hearts, we enter into the true fulfillment of our soul's purpose.

How do we do it? What are the actions we take to utilize these great laws to bring forth the life we want? How do we love, seek guidance, and establish a relationship with our spiritual nature? The bottom line of all the Universal Laws is that simple teaching given so long ago:

"Love one another."

Notes

Chapter 1
The Universal Laws

1. Gandhi, M.K. *Gandhi: An Autobiography,* 1957, Boston, MA: Beacon Press, p. 28.

2. All quotes so marked are Edgar Cayce readings copyrighted by the Edgar Cayce Foundation. For explanation of reading markings, see preliminary note: "Usage of the Edgar Cayce Readings."

3. McArthur, B., *Your Life: Why It Is the Way It Is and What You Can Do About It,* 1993, Virgina Beach, VA: A.R.E. Press, p.5.

Chapter 3
The Law of Love

1. Canfield, J., Hansen, M.V., *Chicken Soup for the Soul,* 1993, Deerfield Beach, FL: Health Communications, Inc., pp. 3-4.

2. Cut-Thru is a registered trademark of the Institute of HeartMath.

3. Tiller, W., R. McCraty, and M. Atkinson, "Toward cardiac coherence: A new noninvasive measure of autonomic system order." *Alternative Therapies,* 1996. 2(1): pp. 52-65. McCraty, R., et al., "The effects of emotions on short-term heart rate variability using power spectrum analysis." *American Journal of Cardiology,* 1995, 76: pp. 1089-1093.

4. Ibid.

5. Freeze-Frame is a registered trademark of the Institute of HeartMath.

6. Tiller, W., et al., "Toward cardiac coherence," op. cit., pp. 52-65.

Chapter 4
Attunement

1. *New York Post* (Nov. 28, 1972). Excepted from Peterson, R., *Everyone Is Right,* 1986, Marina del Rey, CA: DeVorss & Co., p. 184.

2. © 1993 Institute of HeartMath.

3. See readings 257-85 and 333-1.

4. Cady, Dr. Emilie, *Lessons in Truth,* Unity Village, MO: Unity Books, p. 79.

5. See reading 262-89.

6. Peterson, R., *Everyone Is Right,* 1986, Marina del Rey, CA: DeVorss & Co., p.173.

Chapter 5
How to Love

1. Montessori, M., *The Secret of Childhood,* 1970, Notre Dame, IN: Fides Publishers.

2. Tiller, W., et al., "Toward cardiac coherence," op. cit., pp. 52-65.

3. Ibid.

4. Childre, D.L., Freeze-Frame®, *Fast Action Stress Relief,* 1994, Boul-

der Creek, CA: Planetary Publications, p. 27.

5. McCraty, R., Tiller, W., and M. Atkinson, "Head-heart entrainment: A preliminary survey," Institute of HeartMath, pp. 1-9.

6. Paddison, S., *Hidden Power of the Heart*, 1992, Boulder Creek, CA: Planetary Publications, pp. 160-161.

Chapter 6
The Law of Giving

1. Childre, D.L., *CUT-THRU®*, 1996, Boulder Creek, CA: Planetary Publications, p. 80.

2. McArthur, B., op. cit., p. 147.

3. Brother Lawrence, *Practice of the Presence of God*, 1980, Westwood, NJ: Fleming H. Revell Co.

Chapter 7
Freedom Through Forgiveness

1. Peterson, R., op. cit., p.11.

Chapter 8
The Law of Wisdom

1. Fillmore, C., *The Twelve Powers of Man*, 1995, Unity Village, MO: Unity School of Christianity, pp. 90-91.

2. Ibid, p. 90.

3. *A Search for God, Book I*, 1970, Virginia Beach, VA: A.R.E. Press, pp. 33-34.

4. Paddison, S., op. cit., pp.17-18.

5. Wakester, A., "Helen Ellington, A Profile," *The A.R.E. Journal*, 1984, July/August, Virginia Beach, VA: A.R.E. Press.

6. See reading 2533-1.

7. See reading 1158-5.

8. Mother Teresa of Calcutta, *The Love of Christ: Spiritual Counsels*, p. 7.

9. *Daily Word*, Unity Village, MO 64065: Unity Books.

10. Freeman, J.D., *The Story of Unity*, 1997, Unity Village: Unity School of Christianity, pp. 52-53.

Chapter 9
The Master Law of Relationships

1. Butterworth, E., *Discover the Power Within You*, 1968, New York, NY: Harper and Row, p. 144.

2. Peterson, R., op. cit., pp. 74-75.

3. See reading 3661-1.

4. Childre, D.L., *Self-Empowerment: The Heart Approach to Stress Management*, 1992, Boulder Creek, CA: Planetary Publications, p. 40.

5. Rein, G., R.M. McCraty, and M. Atkinson, "Effects of positive and negative emotions on salivary IgA." *Journal for the Advancement of Medicine*, 1995, 8(2): pp. 87-105.

6. Childre, D.L., *Cut-Thru*®, op. cit., pp. 48-63.

7. Ibid., pp. 48-49.

8. Childre, D.L., *Speed of Balance: A Musical Adventure for Emotional and Mental Regeneration,* 1995, Planetary Productions: Boulder Creek, CA.

9. Childre, D.L., *Cut-Thru*®, op. cit., pp. 80-84.

Chapter 10
The Law of Faith

1. Paddison, S., op. cit., pp. 173-175.

2. Rein, G., R.M. McCraty, "Modulation of DNA by coherent heart frequencies," *International Society for the Study of Subtle Energies and Energy Medicine,* 1993, Third Annual Conference, pp. 58-60.

3. Witherspoon, T.E., *Myrtle Fillmore, Mother of Unity,* 1977, Unity Village: Unity Books, pp. 41-43.

4. Gunas: "Bonds that bind the undying dweller imprisoned in the body. (Bhagavad Gita, see 47).

5. *Song of God, Bhagavad Gita.* Translated by Sqami Prabhavananda and Isherweed, C., Mintor Books, ch. 14. Excerpted from Peterson, R., op. cit., p. 148.

Chapter 11
Attunement Through Mercy and Balance

1. Lao Tsu, *Tao Te Ching* © by Feng, G., English, J., 1972, New York: Vintage Books, #2.

Chapter 12
The Laws of One, Enlightenment, and Becoming

1. Peterson, R., op. cit., p. 42.

2. Lao Tsu, op. cit., #35.

3. See readings 5149-1 and 5142-1.

4. Bucke, R. M., *Cosmic Consciousness,* New York, NY: E.P. Dutton and Company, p. 3.

Chapter 13
Grace

1. See readings 2812-1, 2448-2, 1449-1, 1971-1, 987-4, and Butterworth, E., op. cit., p. 39.

2. Sparrow, L., *Reincarnation: Claiming Your Past, Creating Your Future,* 1995, Virginia Beach, A.R.E. Press, pp. 124-125.